Thomas Adolphus Trollope

Giulio Malatesta

A Novel

Thomas Adolphus Trollope

Giulio Malatesta
A Novel

ISBN/EAN: 9783337027803

Printed in Europe, USA, Canada, Australia, Japan

Cover: Foto ©Thomas Meinert / pixelio.de

More available books at **www.hansebooks.com**

GIULIO MALATESTA

A Novel.

BY

T. ADOLPHUS TROLLOPE,

AUTHOR OF

"LA BEATA," "MARIETTA," &c.

IN THREE VOLUMES.

VOL. III.

SECOND EDITION.

LONDON:

CHAPMAN AND HALL, 193, PICCADILLY.

1863.

CONTENTS OF VOL. III.

BOOK IV.

(CONTINUED.)

THE URSULINES AT MONTEPULCIANO.

BOOK V.

SANTA CROCE.

BOOK VI.

THE MARCHESE MALATESTA.

GIULIO MALATESTA.

BOOK IV.

(CONTINUED.)

THE URSULINES AT MONTEPULCIANO.

GIULIO MALATESTA.

CHAPTER VI.

A TÊTE-À-TÊTE IN THE SACRISTY.

It is probable, as has been hinted, that the ecclesiastical superiors who had selected Sister Maddalena for promotion from the remote convent at Ascoli, to be the Superior of the Ursulines of Santa Filomena at Montepulciano, had done so with the intention of refreshing with a certain modicum of greatly-needed new wine those old bottles of theirs, which had become terribly musty under the *régime* of immobility, which was now beginning to be shaken. But that pouring in of new wine under such circumstances is a difficult and dangerous experiment, which we know on high authority is little likely to answer the purpose intended. And it seemed likely in the case in question that the attempt would issue in a catastrophe analogous to that mentioned in the sacred parable.

The fermentation caused by this new wine in the old Montepulciano bottles, seemed likely to be greater than the strength of them could stand. Innovation and heresy are to many minds almost synonymous terms. And there are various departments of orthodoxy in which the instinct that prompts this feeling is not a delusive one. The old nuns in the Ursuline convent were not far wrong in thinking that change of any kind in their ways, practices, and habits, was dangerous to them; as change of habits of life mostly is to the old and infirm.

It is not to be wondered at, therefore, that a spirit of disaffection and insubordination was ripe in the convent under the new rule. And absolute as is the theory of conventual obedience, and high as is the notion we outsiders especially are apt to entertain of the unlimited power of the Superior of a religious house, it is an absolutism difficult to be maintained—like other absolutisms—in the face of a disaffection at all general among the subjects of it.

It was a few days after the discontented members of the community had been scandalised anew by the unheard-of strangeness of the Holy Mother having been closeted with a pensioner of the house during an entire morning, that a more orthodox and less unexampled *tête-à-tête* took place in the sacristy of the convent chapel, at the pleasant evening hour before the Ave Maria. The parties were Sister Giuseppa and the Reverend Domenico Tondi, the Chancellor of the Diocese; and their confidential conversation was an altogether warrantable, orthodox, and correct proceeding. For, was not the Reverend Domenico Tondi also the "Director" of the Ursulines of Santa Filomena? And was not Sister Giuseppa the Vice-Superior of the convent, no new disposition having been as yet taken by the new Abbess to place any other in her stead in that position?

The sacristy in which these two persons were sitting was a snug-looking room enough, though somewhat gloomy, except when the setting sun sent an illuminating gleam athwart it, through the one window placed so high in the wall as to afford no view of the convent garden on which it opened. It was entirely lined from floor to ceiling with a series of dark walnut-wood presses in double tier, the centre of the doors of which were ornamented with large round brass knobs, rubbed up, as well as the shining wood around them, to a perfect polish. There were two breaks only besides the window in the continuity of this polished walnut-wood lining. One opposite to the window extended in a strip, some five feet wide from floor to ceiling, and was occupied by a large crucifix above, and by a massive faldstool beneath it. The other uncovered space of wall extended only half the height of the apartment from the floor, the range of presses being carried on without interruption above it. And the space thus left was occupied by a little conduit of red marble, with a water-cock above it, and a long circular towel on a roller by its side. There were two doors, also of walnut-wood, and so made as to form to the eye no interruption to the range of presses. Both of them were in one corner of the room. One opened on to the little church, and the other on to a corridor communicating with the interior of the convent. In the middle of the room was a large, oblong, massive table, the space beneath which, instead of being void, save for the legs of it, after the fashion of ordinary tables, was filled up with a series of large drawers. The top of the table was covered with a green baize cloth. There were three or four straight-backed, square-made armchairs, with ancient stamped leather seats and backs, fairly indicating them to be at least three hundred years old; and there was an old contemporary of theirs—a large and handsome brass brazier, resting on an iron tripod, the admirable ornamentation of which unmistakably declared its *cinquecentista* origin.

The declining sun, as the closing day approached

the Ave Maria, shot a mellow golden ray through the high window, which lay like a great glistening stripe across the threadbare green baize top of the huge table; sparkled on the brass of the brazier, played on the polished panel of the opposite wall in a strange variety of high lights and demi-lights and shadows, and concentrated itself on the burnished brazen knob in the centre of it with an intensity that made it appear like a ball of fire. The great crucifix was left in deep shadow, as were also the two occupants of the room, who sat side by side near one end of the table; and by virtue of the strikingly characterised harmony of their appearance with the locality and all the objects around them, formed a group which might well be called picturesque, though it could not be said to possess any of the elements of the beautiful.

The tall, gaunt figure, the hard features, and black brows of Sister Giuseppa, are already known to the reader. Don Domenico Tondi, the Chancellor of the Diocese and Director of the Convent, was a dried-up little man, with a head and face of a triangular form, with a minimum of brain packed into the apex, and a maximum of animalism distending the base, across the whole extent of which a wide, lipless mouth, cut like that of a toad, was stretched from corner to corner, so near the lower side of the triangle as to leave scarcely any room for a chin. Close under this strange wide and short lower jaw, came the rim of his ecclesiastical collar, which was of so nearly the same yellow as the whole of his face, that it needed a close glance to see where the dirty skin ended and the dirty linen began. The huge shoes on his feet, much larger, apparently, than necessary, would hardly have offended the ideas of St. Chrysostom upon that subject. The curiously coarse worsted stockings above them were not darned, but pieced with fragments of brown cloth; and the black camlet garment next above them was almost entirely hidden, as he sat, by a blue checked cotton handkerchief, much begrimed with snuff, laid across his knees. His cloth waistcoat was also grimy from the same cause from top to bottom.

"That makes five clear sins, of which four are decidedly grave, and two of them probably mortal," said Don Domenico, ticking off the bill on the fingers of his left hand, while he held a pinch of his favourite dust between the thumb and forefinger of his right; "and three opportunities of cardinal virtues neglected!" He was speaking of the short-comings of the new Abbess, according to Sister Giuseppa's report of her conduct, the particulars of which he had been sorting, tariffing, and labelling *secundum artem*, with the above result.

"Oh! we are not at the end yet, most excellent

father! There are things which your holy conscience would never dream of, and which I could never bring myself to repeat, if it were not for the glory of God and the credit of the house," rejoined Sister Giuseppa, crossing herself as she spoke.

"Eh!" said Don Domenico, sharply, suddenly arresting in his newly-awakened interest the hand which was conveying to his nose a pinch of snuff; "in our position, my dear sister in Christ, it is our bounden duty to allow no scruples of delicacy to interfere with perfect openness between us. I will look the other way, dear sister, while you communicate the facts," added the Director, courteously offering the old woman his snuff-box as he spoke.

Sister Giuseppa took as large a pinch as her finger and thumb would hold, and savoured it leisurely with upturned nose, before she replied, advancing her mouth towards his ear, and hissing out the terrible word, "Heresy! *padre mio!* a clear case of heresy!"

"Oh—h—h!" said Don Domenico, with an accent of disappointment in his tone; "heresy! Heresy, is it? Humph! Heresy, my good Giuseppa, is a malady of which it needs, perhaps, greater skill than yours to read the symptoms."

"I am but a poor nun, your reverence," said the old woman, evidently nettled at the small effect her communication had produced, "but I haven't served the Lord for upwards of half a century without learning to know the savour of heresy when it comes near me! A pure conscience and zeal for the glory of God will stand in the place of book-learning!"

"No doubt! no doubt! What is the case, my excellent sister in Christ?" asked the Director.

"Why! what does your reverence think of her forbidding us to avail ourselves of the holy privileges and dispensation you, yourself, in the exercise of your known discretion and exalted piety, have deigned to procure for this holy house? What do you think of that? If that be not a questioning of the dispensing power of our Holy Father, I should like to know what is! And if any devout and lowly-minded Christian cannot smell heresy there, more shame and pity for them; that is all I say!"

"And you say very well, my sister in Christ! excellently well!" returned the Director. "This new Superior," he continued, inhaling a great pinch of snuff, and nodding his head slowly up and down, "must be one of that sort—a very dangerous and pestilential sort, indeed! But, my dear sister, it is necessary to be prudent in these cases,—it is necessary to be very prudent! We live in bad times,—in bad and strange times, Sister Giuseppa! There is backsliding and lukewarmness in high places! The world is not what it was! And—God forbid that I should speak or even think evil of those placed in spiritual authority over me! and I would not say such a thing for the world!—only to you, Sister Giuseppa, who are a prudent, a God-fearing woman, I may say—between ourselves, you know, quite between ourselves—that our own Bishop here is but a poor creature! I pity him with all my heart, in a position in which knowledge, judgment, energy, zeal, are required. For he is an excellent, worthy man! but the vainest, weakest, shallowest creature!—no learning! less industry! *And* so worldly and self-seeking!—We live in bad times, sister!"

"Ah! bad times indeed! *caro mio padre.* I remember when Monsignore came here ten years ago—it will be eleven years next Nativity of the Blessed Virgin—I said at the time—though I always speak of the right reverend father with that respect which his holy office demands, and even with reverence—(for you cannot expect more from any one than the Holy Spirit has given him)—I said at the time that it seemed strange, and, as it were, a refusal of the blessings of Providence, to bring a stranger to the diocese, when we had among us one so well fitted in every way for the position as Don Domenico Tondi, I said. Things would have been different in Montepulciano, and in this house, if those above us had seen with my eyes!"

"God's will be done!" ejaculated the Director, with a shrug and a grimace, which seemed to add an expression of "since there's no help for it!" to the pious sentiment.

"Ah! God's will be done!" re-echoed the nun, holding out her fingers towards the priest's snuff-box, in a manner that compelled the offer of another pinch.

"But there was one thing, *carissimo mio padre*, which afflicted me, God forgive me for it, even more grievously than her very evident and most pestilent heresy! She has strictly forbidden that devout woman, our cook, Guglielmina, to make any more of those little confections and patties which your reverence and one or two others of the good friends of the house were so fond of! She has positively refused to allow any more to be sent from the convent to any one! under pretence that whatever we can spare from our slender revenues ought to be employed in a different manner! Oh! It is very abominable."

"It is the will of the Lord to try us, my sister!" ejaculated the priest, while a heavy scowl passed over his features. "But as for this shameless woman, what you tell me is certainly a sin against the holy virtue of charity, and I am very much inclined to think," he added, tapping his snuff-box as he spoke, "at least constructively a sin against the Holy Spirit!"

"No! you don't say so!" exclaimed Sister Giuseppa, with a gleam of gratified malice in her eye. "Ah! your reverence, it is you who are a great theologian! *Ma proprio un peccato contra lo Spirito Santo!*"* she added, throwing up her head, as she savoured her pinch of snuff and her odium theologicum together with exquisite gusto, "who would have thought it! But that is what it is to be a profound canonist!"

"Mind! I said *constructively*, Sister Giuseppa, constructively! And I am free to own that such is my opinion. But *che vuole?* What would you have? We live in degenerate times! Still something ought to be done. It is very monstrous!"

"Surely, your reverence, in your position, and with your immense science, will be able to take some steps for the protection of our poor house!—you, my father, who, after the blessed St. Ursula and the holy Filomena," said Sister Giuseppa, crossing herself in compliment to the two first-named patrons, and with a leer of holy coaxing to

* "But really a sin against the Holy Spirit." *Really* hardly expresses the full force of the "proprio," which involves a "Come! really now! you don't say that," sort of meaning.

the third, "have ever been our protector and most efficacious patron!"

"We must see what is to be done!" replied the Director; "we must consider what steps can be taken. In the mean time, be vigilant, Sister Giuseppa! This holy house, and I may say the Church, expect it at your hands! Keep a strict and holy watch! And perhaps you may be able —you understand——"

"Trust me to keep my eyes open, your reverence! Trust old Sister Giuseppa—a simple nun —to do her part!"

"But caution!" said the priest, holding up a black-nailed forefinger in front of his snuffy nose, and sinking his voice to a whisper; "caution and vigilance!"

"*A chi lo dice!*" returned the nun. "I shall have the advantage of speaking with your paternity again ere long?"

"Assuredly! assuredly! my sister in Christ! Ah! if certain folks had had the holy discernment to place you at the head of this house——!"

"Oh! *reverendissimo padre!* If it had but pleased the Lord so to illuminate the hearts of princes, as that your reverence should have been put in the place that was due to you——!"

"*A rivederci dunque, sorella mia!*" * said the

* "Au revoir, my sister."

Director, as he passed out of the sacristy by the door leading to the church, giving his benediction as he went by the usual flourish of his dirty fingers.

"*A rivederci, riverenza!*" returned the nun, bowing lowly, with her arms crossed upon her bosom.

Before the Director had been gone an hour, Sister Giuseppa had found an opportunity of whispering her great news into the sympathising ear of Sister Maria:

"I have had a long conversation with our Director, sister!—such a consoling conversation! The holy man places great confidence in me!"

"In whom better could he place confidence, Sister Giuseppa! And what does his paternity say?"

"Sister Maria! we have a Superior who has been guilty of sin against the Holy Spirit!" said the other, hissing the words into the ear of her hearer.

"Holy Virgin and gracious St. Ursula keep and preserve us!" exclaimed Sister Maria, crossing herself ever so many times in rapid succession.

"Hush—h—h! Prudence, Sister Maria! The Director recommends to us the utmost prudence! Yes! a clear case of sin against the Holy Spirit!" replied Sister Giuseppa, repeating the words with an infinite relish. "Nothing less than that! What do you think of it? Oh! he is a great theologian, our blessed Director!"

"It is very dreadful, Sister Giuseppa!"

"Ah! horrible, Sister Maria! But a very blessed thing, and a great grace of the Virgin, that it should be discovered! I thought as much when I laid the facts before his paternity. Oh! I knew there was something very bad! But, prudence, Sister Maria!"

"*A chi lo dite!* Sister Giuseppa."

And so, before the same hour on the following evening, a mysterious whisper had passed through all the community, and every member of it was aware that some almost unmentionable horror had been providentially discovered with reference to the new Abbess! And the nuns were seizing every opportunity of getting into corners by twos and threes, to ask and tell rumours, and communicate ideas respecting the terrible news. And before long the great question which divided the opinions of the sisterhood was, whether the new Abbess would be burned within the convent walls, or on the principal piazza of the city.

CHAPTER VII.

THE ABBESS AND HER PUPIL.

It soon became impossible for the Abbess to avoid observing that there was something amiss between her and the members of the sisterhood under her government, and that their sentiments with regard to her were not such as were desirable. Nevertheless, as the Director's injunctions as to "caution" and "prudence" were observed most sedulously, she was wholly at a loss for any explanation of the unpleasant symptoms which forced themselves on her notice. Least of all did it occur to her to imagine that her intercourse with one of the young persons placed under her special care could form any part of the grounds of discontent with her government of the convent. And it was inevitable that what had passed between her and

Stella at their last interview should make that intercourse closer and still more confidential for the future. The tie which henceforth bound them together was far too strong an one to be severed or weakened by the etiquette of convent discipline, even if either of them had been aware of the extent to which they were considered to be sinning against it. Henceforward for ever the heart-life of these two women was to be centred in one and the same individual. Their hopes, fears, and interests were, of course, the same, their wishes identical; and the goal, which represented to the ardent imagination of the younger the full attainment of all that earth had to offer of happiness, could not but shine out as a dim distant star to the resuscitated heart of the elder, like the nascent glimmering of the possibility of a joy in that future, where till now all had been dead, arid, and barren as the desert.

But it would have been a curious study, not so much of the innate differences between one human temperament and another, as between the results of different courses of life-discipline on the subjects of them, to mark the differences in the effect produced by the discovery they had both of them made on these two women.

Stella Altamari had received from nature a stronger moral fibre, a greater power of volition, and a bolder temperament, than Maddalena Tacca. Youth, moreover, is bolder and more sanguine than advanced life. Yet more is a heart which has grown in the world's sunshine braver than one which has known only its cold shade. But greatest difference of all between those two in the capacity of hopefulness, in the elasticity which can rise from the depression of past sorrows to fresh struggles and new aims, was that which resulted from the twenty years of living death which had made half the existence of the latter. A distant glimmering of the possibility of a feeling of joy had been manifested, as has been said, to the resuscitated heart of the woman who had been so long in her moral grave. But resuscitation is never otherwise than painful. The surest mark of the intensity of suffering is the limitation of the sufferer's desires to absolute repose, and the cessation of all sensation. The moral nature cleaves to moral life, and abominates moral death with as strong an instinct as the physical body abhors physical death. And the heart may suffer much, and turn eagerly at nature's kindly and beneficent prompting to new hopes and aims. But the heart which has suffered most is that which limits its aspirations to the moral death of absolute vacancy; which dreads a new affection even as the quivering nerves dread another turn of the tormentor's screw;

which has learned to distrust life so profoundly, that it clings to the numbed immobility of annihilation.

This was the condition of heart and mind in which the discovery made by Stella and herself had found the Abbess. Twenty years ago her babe had been torn from her bosom, and she had been consigned to a grave where it appeared impossible that any further tidings of him should reach her. If any half-conscious hope had lingered for a while in her heart, it had long since perished. And now the numbed heart was to be wakened from its long trance, the blood was to tingle again in its old currents, the pulses to be set beating afresh! A strange fear and trembling, like that which prisoners have felt when called, after long, long years of confinement in dark cells, to come forth into the light of day, fell upon the Abbess when the possibilities of the future shaped themselves in her mind.

Stella saw only cause of unmixed delight in the discovery she had made! What a joy for Giulio! His mother found! and such a mother! And *she* had been the discoverer! Oh! the pleasure of instantly writing her great tidings! There would be no difficulty in sending her letter now! She should be the means of bringing the long lost son and long lost mother to each other's arms! And, of course, with such an aid on her side as the Abbess, her family would soon be brought to hear reason!

Poor little sanguine Stella was doomed, therefore, to a painful shock of disappointment when she was called to her next interview with the Superior. She had been a good deal surprised that this call had not come on the very next day. Was it possible to suppose that the Abbess could be aught but overjoyed at the discovery! Then occurred to her mind a horrible suspicion that the discovery of her son's attachment to her might be as displeasing to the Abbess as the finding of her son must be a source of unmixed rejoicing. At all events, did she not want to hear a thousand things which only she, Stella, could tell her?

She little guessed, nor could have understood, had it been told her, that every hour of the intervening time had been passed by the Abbess between dread of and longing for the conversation for which the younger and stronger heart was so eager! that she had been nerving herself for the interview with fear and trembling!

At last the summons came. And Stella found the Abbess seated exactly as she had been on the former occasions. But even her young eye perceived at once that she was changed. She had been pallid, subdued in manner, and even sad in accent and in bearing. But she had not been beaten down as she seemed now, when Stella fancied that she ought to be rejoicing in the great glad tidings that had so unexpectedly come to her. Her eyes seemed sunken in her head, and her face swollen with weeping, and there was a languor of hopelessness in the droop of her head upon her bosom which was very different from the quiet, graceful dignity of her previous bearing.

She got up, however, as Stella entered the room, and advancing a step from her chair to meet her, took her head in her hands, and, pressing it against her bosom, kissed her on the forehead.

"Sit down, my daughter! we have much, very much, to say to each other—much that each of us must be so eager to hear!"

"And, in truth, dearest mother," Stella could not abstain from saying, "I had hoped to have been called to your presence sooner!"

"No doubt! no doubt! my child. And I ought to have considered your natural impatience more. But—Stella—I am but a poor broken creature. I have been much shaken——"

"But it must have been a great joy to you, my mother, to have found—we may call it found—your lost son, and such a son, my mother!"

"Yes! dearest Stella! a great, a fearful joy!"

The Abbess had never before made use of so

loving a mode of address in speaking to her, and Stella was encouraged by it to say:

"And the joy is not diminished, dearest mother, by the knowledge that the son thus discovered loves me?"

"Dear child!" replied the Abbess, placing her hand affectionately on Stella's head, "assuredly the joy is not diminished,—but the fear is increased!"

"Why should there be fear at all, my mother?" asked Stella, after a short pause, during which she had been endeavouring, unsuccessfully, to fathom the Abbess's meaning.

"My Stella! Can you ask such a question! What fear? Yet it is natural that it should appear so to your mind! You know not what it is to have ——but, at any rate, my Stella, you must be aware of the difficulties that are before us as regards the attachment of you and——Giulio for each other?"

"But if I—if we have your approbation, my mother, that is a difficulty the less, not a difficulty the more in our path."

"How so, my child?"

"You will not lend your aid, my mother, to enforce upon me the terrible alternative of a marriage with the Marchese Alfonso, or the taking of the veil. You will support me in refusing at least the latter fate, will you not, my mother?"

"That, in any case, I should have done to the best of my power, my daughter. But, alas! what can that power avail? There are other convents, even if the Canon Altamari should not prefer using his influence to place a new Superior in this."

"But surely, my mother, it would be difficult to insist on my becoming a nun after one Superior had declined to admit me to profession because I had openly declared that I had no vocation for that state!" urged Stella.

"And would it add, think you, my child, to my authority on the subject, when it became known that your object in refusing the veil was to marry and confer your large possessions on the son of the Abbess who pronounced you unfitted for the vows?"

"But you will not give me up, my mother! You would not stand by and see me forced against my will into a cloister!" pleaded Stella, who was already beginning to lose some of the golden illusions with which the discovery of—as it seemed to her hopes—a mother-in-law in the Abbess had inspired her.

"I fear me, my dear child, that the discovery we have made may have the effect of increasing the difficulties before you, and not diminishing them! My heart misgives me that it may be so.

And for that reason—mainly for that reason—I have felt terrified at that which is before us! Think you, my child, that it will help your hopes, when it shall be found out that he who asks your hand is the son of a cloistered nun!"

"But we knew before—Giulio was till now motherless. And—and—the circumstances under which you—were separated from him——"

"I fear, my poor child, that you do not understand the rules and principles which govern the world in such matters!" said the Abbess, with a heavy sigh.

"At all events, my mother, there will be the great, great happiness for Giulio and for you! And for the rest, Giulio will know what is best to be done. At all events, he will come here! I shall see him! I am sure that all will then be well!"

"My child! my child! you make me tremble! Bethink yourself a little, Stella!"

And, in fact, the Abbess was alarmed and almost aghast at Stella's eagerness, and sanguine persuasion that all they had to do was to cry aloud from the house-top the discovery they had made. During the long hours of the days and nights since the previous interview with Stella, she had been painfully meditating on the future, and on the course which it would be wisest and best to pursue. Her heart yearned to her child. The maternal instincts which had so long lain dead beneath the pall of conventual moral lethargy, had been powerfully aroused. But it was still to the babe that had been taken from her bosom that her heart and her imagination turned. And it seemed to her feelings as if it were but a false and delusory gratification of her maternal yearning to bring a bearded man to her in the place of the babe she had lost. Then there were doubts and fears of a more reasoned sort. Should she not be bringing evil to her son by the discovery of herself? He had made his way to a prosperous and honourable position in the world. Would not the knowledge that his mother was an unmarried cloistered nun be a sore disadvantage to him? Would such knowledge be welcome to him? Would his filial feeling be strong enough to stand against the sentiment with which we are apt to regard those who are injurious and inconvenient to us? Might she not, by making herself known to her son, be going in quest of new heart-laceration and the re-opening of long-closed wounds? Had she the courage to face all these risks? Would unbiased wisdom counsel her to do so?

And all these meditations had led her to the issue to which similar doubts and fears usually bring timid and irresolute doubters. At all events, it would be best to wait—not to be too precipitate

—to feel the way—to sound the mind of her son. She would have the means of doing this effectually by the co-operation of Stella. By degrees he might be prepared for the revelation. Then, again, as to his and Stella's attachment. It could hardly be but that the precipitate disclosure of her secret would make their difficulties greater. She saw but small hope for them in any case. She had not sufficient knowledge of the world to be fully aware of the violence of the opposition that would of course be made to such a marriage as that between a fortuneless captain in the Piedmontese service and the richest heiress in Tuscany. But she knew that the lady's family objected, and she had an exaggerated notion of the power of a great and wealthy family.

The more she looked at the matter in every point of view, the more she felt that it would be the height of imprudence to divulge the secret prematurely; and that, at all events, the doing so would require the courage and decision of which she was not capable. And she was, in truth, terrified at finding that Stella had no other idea on the subject than the promptest and most unhesitating revelation of the truth.

"Trust me, my dear child," she continued, "you do not appreciate duly the results of such a discovery! What possibilities may lie in the future for bringing to pass an union between you and my unfortunate son, I cannot say! But this I am sure of, that the difficulties you have to contend with would be increased by the secret we have discovered being prematurely divulged."

"Why unfortunate?" cried Stella, who had raised her head with a sharp, defiant sort of movement at the word.

"Why unfortunate, dearest? Can you ask? Why is *my* son unfortunate? Is it no misfortune to have *me* for a mother?"

"I would rather say, my mother, that you are fortunate in having him for a son!"

"May you never, never know, my daughter, what it is to feel that you have injured the being you best love by the mere fact of having brought him into the world!"

"Mother," said Stella, after a pause, "to my thinking you are led by the sufferings you have endured to exaggerate the evil you deplore. Where there has been no sin—pardon my great presumption in speaking to you so—it seems to me as if there cannot be any such insuperable cause for regret. Think, only think!" she added, with a *naïve* intensity of earnestness which would have been amusing to any third party who could have overheard her, "of the loss, if he had never been born at all! Think of the loss to his country—to

Italy, my mother!"—"to me specially," she would have said, "and to all the human race in the second place," if she had spoken her entire thought.

Little attuned as was the mind of the Abbess to any pleasant thought, she could not help smiling, with a feeling of pleasure, at Stella's innocent enthusiasm. He had had the fortune, at all events, then, of making his own the priceless love of one true and exceedingly lovely and loving heart—this unfortunate son of hers! If only he was better worthy of it than his father!

"Tell me, then, my Stella," said the Abbess, looking at her fondly—"tell me something about this paladin, whose non-existence would have been such a loss to his country—and perhaps to some individual citizen—or citizen*ess* besides?"

"How can I describe him to you, my mother," replied Stella, dropping the silken lashes over her eyes, and with an indescribable manifestation of pleasure in the task assigned her, which might be likened to the purring of a happy kitten. "It is not only what he has done—though it is well known that the important success at Curtatone was mainly due to him—and I could tell you many another deed of his besides—and some day I must tell you, for he never will!—and it is not that he is handsome—though I confess I never saw any other nearly so beautiful!—it is—I think it is—a sort of noble gentleness that is in his heart, and shines out of his eyes! I think it is mainly that, which goes straight to one's heart! And I will tell you an observation that I have made," she continued, with an obviously ingenuous pouring out of the most secret meditations of her little heart; "we are taught, you know, my mother, that to love God purifies and elevates the heart and soul. And I have observed that my love for Giulio has produced similar effects on my character. I am better —better in heart and in mind since I have loved him! It has given me higher and nobler thoughts and feelings, and larger charity towards all others! I think even that I am less silly and giddy than I was before! I think, if one loved a man who was not good, one would become worse than before. I am sure that the effect my love for Giulio has had on me must show that he is very God-like!"

"Stella!"

"Of course I do not mean like God, my mother; but that he has qualities of the same kind as those which we attribute to God. Then he is so beloved by all who know him. To hear his fellow-students at the University speak of him! He saved the lives of more than one of them at the risk of his own! And if others had not told me of the facts, I should never have known them! Oh! my mother; believe me, let what may have been the past, a mother who has come to the discovery that she possesses such a son, should not think herself unfortunate!"

"You are an eloquent eulogist, my Stella," said the Abbess, with a sad, yet pleased smile; "now tell me, if you have condescended to remember any such unimportant details, something of the appearance of this handsomest man you ever saw."

"If I remember! Oh, *madre mia*, if I were a painter, I could paint his portrait here just as well as if he were sitting to me for it!" answered Stella, closing her eyes, and revelling in the mental image she had summoned from that storehouse of the imagination, where it dwelt continually within call at the shortest notice. "I am afraid you will think that I want to flatter you, my mother," she said, with a smiling glance at the face of the Abbess, "if, after all I have said, I tell you that he is like you. But he is so—to a certain degree. He has the same regular oval face, and the same nose. The mouth, too, is like; but the chin is different, larger and more square. His hair is certainly the most beautiful that ever was seen! Dark, dark brown; nearly, but not quite, black; and lying on his head in great thick glossy curls!—oh! such beautiful hair. The forehead, again, is like yours, my mother! high and large, and very white. But the most beautiful, the most wonderful of all, are the eyes! They are eyes that nature must have intended for somebody that was to be born dumb! For they seem to be able to supply the place of speaking. They are sometimes very pensive, thoughtful eyes, and sometimes quick and flashing as the lightning! They are very fierce eyes! and they are such tender eyes—oh! so tender! They can be stern and commanding eyes; but I have seen them so beseeching—so beseeching, that no human being could say, No, to them. And I can tell you, *madre mia*, that they are eyes that cannot help telling all his secrets! Such tell-tale eyes! They told me that he loved me long before his tongue did! But that is a secret between ourselves, *madre mia!* I never told him that his eyes had turned traitors and blabbed, what he never ordered them to tell! And I know for certain, that what these eyes tell, is the truth; they cannot tell lies," added Stella, sententiously.

"There have been beautiful eyes, which could speak eloquently, and which could tell lies!" said the Abbess, with a sigh.

"But they must have been different!" said Stella, with prompt decision; "I, too, have seen beautiful eyes, which I would not trust; but *his* are different;—oh! so different! I am sure that nobody could disbelieve them."

"In short, Stella! you love him! And I feel that that is a strong evidence in his favour; for I do not think that *you* would love unworthily!"

"And is it not then an evidence in my favour that he loves me?" rejoined Stella, with illogical *naïveté.*

"That I may possibly be able to answer, my Stella, at some future time," replied the Abbess, shaking her head.

"Some future time, my mother!" re-echoed Stella;—"a time very near at hand, I trust!"

"I know not, my child! It needs much thought. I do not see my way, Stella! I tremble at the thought of taking a step of which I cannot foresee the consequences. If I were to injure Giulio's prospects by the discovery! If he were to feel that his mother had been a second time fatal to him!"

"Trust me, my mother, trust me, who know him, that to throw himself into your arms will be the greatest joy that Giulio could ask from fate! To discover his long lost mother is the great object and enterprise of his life."

"I doubt it not, my child! But that is no guarantee for his contentment when he should discover the mother he has so long sought in a cloistered nun! Still less is it any security against the mischief that such a discovery would cause him in the minds of others!"

It was in vain that Stella strove to combat the fears and misgivings of the Abbess, and inspire her with courage to make herself known at once to her son.

"Give me time, my child! It is a great, a fearful step! Give me time to think! Perhaps you are right, my Stella; but I must have time to think of it maturely."

And this was all that Stella was able to obtain from the shrinking timidity and weakness of the Abbess. The question was debated between them at several subsequent interviews; and it would have been curious to mark how, despite the circumstances of the social relation in which the two women stood towards each other, the stronger, fresher, and bolder mind of the young boarder gradually, and without any purpose on the part of either of them, assumed the position and the task of strengthening, encouraging, and supporting the depressed and unnerved energies of her Superior; —a curious, but not an unpleasing study! For so true and warm an affection grew up between them, and the eagerness of the young and unbroken heart was bent with so transparent a purity of unselfishness on bringing about that which she was convinced would restore a large portion of happiness to the poor crushed coward heart beside her, that the relationship of the two minds resembled that between a child and the aged blind whose steps it tenderly guides.

But Stella's utmost efforts failed to stimulate the Abbess so far as to obtain her consent to the step she was urging on her. Fear had too entirely and permanently ousted hope from any place in that bruised and long lethargic heart. And the utmost that Stella could at length obtain from her was permission to write a letter, which, in very cautious and guarded terms, should in some degree prepare Giulio for the possibility of a discovery. Again and again she wrote, modifying her letter in compliance with the exigencies of the Abbess's fears. At length she induced her half-reluctantly to permit the following letter to be sent :

"At last, at last, my own beloved, there will come up to you from the silence of the cloister a voice from your poor buried Stella ;—a voice bidding you to be of good heart and cheer, my Giulio! —a voice telling you that she is still alive,—I do not mean her body only (for that is not what they try to kill in convents; and in truth I have had nothing to suffer on that score), but her heart, and mind, and soul. These are what they try to kill and bury in these tombs; but have no fear for me, my own! My heart, and mind, and soul are living still. Is it necessary to add that they are all still your own?

"Yet it must be admitted, my Giulio, that these convents are horrible places! The utter isolation is perhaps the most dreadful thing about them. There is absolutely no means of communicating with the outer world. The watchfulness and the precautions taken are such as to render it impossible. I am quite sure that you have been making attempts, my poor Giulio, to communicate with your little buried Stella; but it has caused me no surprise that no word has reached me. I know too well the impossibility of it.

"How then, you will say, can I hope to find the means of making this letter reach you? And that question brings me to the mention of a great event that has happened in this still and monotonous convent existence. Last January old *Madre* Veronica, the Superior to whose care and guidance I was specially consigned, died. And we have a new Mother Superior! The greatest of all possible events in a convent. I will not now speak to you at length about the new Abbess. She is a very different sort of person in every respect from the Mother Veronica; and her kindness has been an infinite comfort to me. It will tell you all, in one word, that it is needful for me to write about her, when I say that I have found in her a kind and loving *friend*. It may seem surprising, perhaps, to your mundane ideas of a convent life, my Giulio, to be told, that it is by no means a matter of course that even the Superior herself should be able to correspond freely with the outside world. Her every act is spied out and commented on; she can do nothing secretly; and if there exist in the community any feeling of ill will towards her, it might be almost as imprudent for her as for any other of the sisterhood to send any unavowable letter out of the convent. From all this you will understand, that even under the present changed circumstances of the convent, it is by no means an easy matter for me to write to you. But an attempt will be made to cause these lines to reach you, because I have something more important to tell you than merely that I love you as dearly as ever;—no, that is a mistake; nothing can be more important than that;—but something which at least will be newer and less well known to you. [The new Superior will lend her aid to the sending of this letter, partly because she herself is in some degree interested in the contents of it.]" (Stella had written this; but the Abbess had insisted on suppressing the passage included between brackets.)

"It will seem strange to you, after all that I have said about the utter isolation of our convent life; but the fact is that, if I am not mistaken, I have come upon a clue which may lead you to the discovery of the mother whose loss you have so long deplored. What if it should turn out that she has lain hid all this time in one of the houses of this order! [Should my suspicion prove to have any foundation of probability—it would be necessary to proceed with caution and discretion.]" (This passage was added at the instance of the Abbess.) "All is very uncertain as yet; and that is why I am compelled, to my great annoyance, to write in such mysterious and unsatisfactory terms. The best mode of proceeding would be for you to come, if possible, hither, and seek an interview with the Abbess; assigning any motive that you may think best. It is not probable that I should be able to see you;—at all events, not otherwise than in the *parlatorio*, under the watchful eyes—and ears—of one of the old nuns. Even that would be very much better than nothing! But even that would be doubtful. The Abbess, however, would see you; and I think that that would be the best method of prosecuting your search for your poor mother. The

Abbess would be prepared to receive you, and to speak on the subject in question.

"Forgive me, my own Giulio, for writing in this mysterious strain! It is not my fault! I am not permitted to do otherwise!

"At all events, the chance is worth something which gives me an opportunity of telling you that I am just as much your own, just as much determined never to give heart or hand to any other, as the first day I came here. They have made no step, my Giulio, towards conquering your little Stella,—not one! I often say myself, this is my Curtatone! And be very sure that I, too, shall be victorious. They won't make me a Captain of Lancers, I am afraid! But I shall fight my battle, AND WIN IT, as well as other folks!

"I saw one of the old charts of the convent the other day; in a printed volume; and at the bottom of it there was a circle, with the words '*locus sigilli*'—the place of the seal, they told me.—Thus —'*locus* ○ *sigilli.*' That is the place, sir; just where I have made the circle.

"Adieu my own, own dearest!

"Your buried but still living

"STELLA."

This letter the Abbess promised to have conveyed

under cover to Francesca Palmiera, near the Porta Romana, Florence.

But it was some time before she succeeded in finding the means of doing so; and though the letter did eventually reach the hands for which it was intended, a further delay occurred before it arrived at its destination.

END OF BOOK IV.

BOOK V.

SANTA CROCE

CHAPTER I.

CAPTAIN MALATESTA'S LETTERS.

Giulio Malatesta received his promotion at the time it had been promised to him. But he was disappointed in his expectation of being able to obtain leave of absence in the course of that year. From month to month the pressing exigencies of the service, which allowed but little relaxation in any kind to the scanty troops of the little Piedmontese army during those disastrous years, made his absence from his regiment impossible. And it was not till the early spring of 1851 that he was at length able to put into execution his long-cherished plan of visiting Bologna, in the hope of finding there some clue to the discovery of his mother.

He had corresponded all this time, more or less

regularly, with Professor Varani, and with Rinaldo Palmieri.

The Professor had promised him that he would make inquiries, with a view to preparing the ground for his proposed investigations. But he had been able to do very little in this way. He gave him carefully, in writing, a detailed statement of the facts respecting the marriage of his mother, which he had already communicated to him by word of mouth at Pisa; and he promised him a letter of introduction to his own mother, Signora Varani, who was still living, now a very old woman, at Bologna. But this was about the extent of what the Professor had been able to contribute to the object in view. The letters which passed between him and Giulio were for the most part filled with political discussions, the general tendency of which was to operate and record the progress of Giulio's conversion from those Giobertinian dreams of a reformed and glorified Papacy, which was to be the leading star of Italy's future progress—dreams which the conduct of the reforming Pope during these years so effectually discredited, that nearly all that younger generation, which had been attracted by the splendour of the Giobertinian Utopia, were convinced of the baseless nature of their vision, save such as at the bottom of their hearts preferred the Papacy to Italy.

The correspondence between Giulio and Rinaldo turned during the earlier portion of it mainly on Rinaldo's love-matters, and his approaching marriage; and during that part of it which was subsequent to that event, had reference to the result of Rinaldo's journey to Montepulciano, and to various schemes for introducing letters into the convent, all of which proved abortive on discussion.

Several letters also had passed between Giulio and his friend Carlo Brancacci. And a few extracts from some of these will suffice as indications of the state of things in the Palazzo Altamari during Stella's banishment at Montepulciano.

In a letter written towards the end of September, 1849, after speaking of the recent return to Florence of his uncle and the Contessa Zenobia, from spending a couple of months at Leghorn, Carlo continued:

"As for myself, I am too thorough a Florentine to find anything very delightful in these migrations to the sea-side, which modern fashion makes so imperative. I am never so contented out of sight of Giotto's tower, as beneath the shadow of it. And I suspect that my uncle is very much of the same way of thinking. But needs must, when the Contessa Zenobia drives! Her ladyship, of course, was in high feather there, on the *Passeggiata dell' Ardenza*,* and down on the Pancaldi baths.† But there is no need of describing to you herself or her ways. And I am sure you have already pictured to yourself that fairy-like form on the extremity of the pier, in very high spirits and very high-heeled boots, and a very high *libeccio* ‡ blowing in from the south-west! I assure you it was a sight to be seen; and you would have laughed, as I have every time I have remembered it, if you had seen my excellent uncle's distress, of body and mind, partly at the *inconvenance* of her ladyship's appearance, partly at the danger of losing his own hat and wig, and partly at his difficulty of maintaining his footing. That animal, the Marchese Alfonso, gave us his company down there part of the time. There is no telling you what a creature it is! I think he is rather frightened—perhaps his provincial propriety is a little scandalised—at La Zenobia. And if it were not for his reverence the Canonico Adalberto, I should not despair of the possibility of making such a breach between

* The Marine Parade of Leghorn.

† The bathing is done at Leghorn in a number of canvas huts, erected on a miniature archipelago of rocks a few yards from the shore. The passages, bridges, and spaces between these, are paved and covered with awnings, and form the resort of the gayer portion of the fashionable Leghorn world.

‡ The wind most prevalent at Leghorn is called the Libeccio.

the little man and the Contessa, as might effectually get rid of him. It is very easy to see that she has the utmost contempt for him. But it is of no use speculating on any such possibilities, worse luck! For the Canonico is not an adversary against whom it is easy to win a game of any description. He is one of those men who wills what he wills in earnest. He is as quiet and gentle in manner as a lamb; and you would think it the easiest thing in the world to turn him round your finger, and bring him to consent to anything. And so it is, as long as the matter in question is nothing that he very particularly cares about. But he means to join the Malatesta to the Altamari property. And it no more matters to him what the human tools are that he has to use in doing the job, so that they are obedient to his hand, than does the colour of the parchment the title-deeds are written on. By-the-by, I am not sure whether I ever told you that no word has been said to the Marchese Alfonso of his having a rival in his pretensions to the hand of the Contessina. I might easily do this; but I have thought, on the whole, that it was best not to say it. It would probably be very easy to frighten the Signor Marchese into abandoning all thoughts of an Altamari marriage—if, again, it were not for the Canonico. But the wretched little man fears him, and not without reason, more than anything else;

and there cannot be the least doubt, that his reverence would find the means of keeping him up to his word."

It another letter, of about a week later date, Carlo wrote:

"Of course, one of my first visits on returning to Florence, was to our friend Rinaldo Palmieri. You know all thé story of his tracking the Contessina and her uncle to Montepulciano. And in truth, it is a great comfort to know where she is! But beyond that we have been able to accomplish nothing. La Signora Francesca, perhaps, might have been permitted to speak with the prisoner in the *parlatorio* of the convent. But she could not have approached within four or five yards of her, and the interview must have taken place under the supervision of one of the nuns. Under these circumstances, we all thought it best not to allow La Signora Francesca to become personally known to the convent authorities. For it might come to pass, that it would be desirable that she should not be recognised as an acquaintance of the Contessina."

In another letter, written about a month later, the following passage occurs:

"If it were not for that terrible Canonico,

we should have an easy game before us. For nothing could be easier than to make an irreparable breach between the Marchese Alfonso and the Contessa. It is evident that she has taken a regular aversion to the poor little creature. They are both equally and inimitably absurd, each in their own way; and the scenes that take place between them would make the fortune of a dozen farces. He is made up of the very quintessence of priggism and insignificance. He is full of a thoroughly provincial notion of his own greatness, genealogical and other, and is utterly astonished and scandalised at our easy-going democratical Florentine indifference to such matters. Then, his old-world provincial dandyism is the most ludicrous thing in the world, and makes him the laughing-stock of all Florence. He is extremely devout, too, you must know, and is much given to make his little church matters and observances the topic of drawing-room conversation, to the infinite disgust of La Zenobia, which she manifests in a way that it is the fun of the world to see! She dares not tell him, what I firmly believe is her own intimate conviction, that a young man has no business with such things, and that she should like him a deal better if he swore like a trooper, and kissed all the girls in the house. But she flounces, and tosses, and kicks, and makes grimaces, in a manner that sometimes tries the nerves of my '*povero zio*' * terribly. One day, when the little Marchesino had been giving us a long account of some anniversary service founded and kept up by some of his family at Fermo, detailing the particulars of the vestments of the priests, and the numbers of the candles, and I know not what, she burst out with, 'For my part, *mon cher*, I should say, with the divine Voltaire, *La messe ne vaut pas la chandelle!*' You know her way of patchworking her scraps of French. The little man looked thunderstruck, as well he might. But, talking of that, she equally astonished a much bigger man, a certain herculean Austrian captain in garrison here, one Von Stoggendorf, a great favourite of hers, by assuring him that he was '*Le cauchemar des dames!*' But I doubt whether he would have understood her much better if she had said '*La coqueluche*,' which, I suppose, was what she meant.

"Adieu, old fellow! Keep up your spirits. We'll floor the Marchese yet, somehow; and you shall win the day in the long run! Perhaps it may be in the design of Providence that the Illustrissimo Signor Canonico Adalberto Altamari may get a touch of gout in the stomach! Who knows!

"Yours always,

"CARLO."

* "Poor uncle."

A passage from another letter, without date, but evidently written some time in the spring of 1850, shows that Giulio did not get his first intimation of the change of Superior at Montepulciano from Stella's letter to him:

"At last, my dear Giulio," Carlo writes, "I have some news to give you from Montepulciano—not, I hasten to say, from the Contessina Stella herself—but still news that may be important, and that can hardly turn out to be otherwise than favourable. The Superior of the convent of Ursulines, one Mother Veronica, to whose charge the Contessina was specially consigned by her precious uncle, died, it seems, very suddenly, last January, and a new Superior has been appointed in her place. Of course we—that is to say, Palmieri and his wife and I—did our best to find out something about the new Abbess. She was brought to Montepulciano, it seems, from some other distant convent of the order. It is said that she is a woman of very different stamp from her predecessor—a person of culture, and, as far as an Abbess can be, of liberal views and tendencies. It is very possible that such a person may refuse to be any party to a scheme for coercing a girl to a hateful marriage by threatening the veil as an alternative. It may be, even, that something better may be hoped from her indulgence and pity. We shall see! The Palmieri are on the look-out, and you may depend on it that no shadow of a chance of communicating with the prisoner shall be suffered to escape. Meantime, it can hardly be doubted that the Contessina's lot must be ameliorated under the rule of such a Superior.

"Our Carnival here has been a very dull one—very different, indeed, from those happy days which we enjoyed together in 1848."

One more extract from a letter, written towards the end of the year, will serve to show the result of those further inquiries which Carlo had, in his former letter, promised his friend should not be neglected:

"Palmieri has picked up some rather strange rumours from Montepulciano, which seem to show that it is probable that the change of Superior, of which I wrote to you in the spring, may affect the Contessina Stella in a manner different from anything I then anticipated. I told you that the new Abbess had the character of being a person of—for an Abbess—liberal tendencies. I suppose that the placing her there was a move made by the influence of those who, just about that time, had their heads full of the notion that the old Lady on the Seven Hills was going to be regenerated, and turn over a new leaf. You remember how often we have talked over that matter in old times in Pisa? I take it you, like the rest of the world, have by this time lost all faith in any such expectation. You know I always thought that any notion of washing the Scarlet Dame white, or even rose-colour, was about as hopeful a speculation as washing a blackamoor white. We all see what the plan has come to in high places; and it would seem that this particular little attempt at Montepulciano has come to grief in a similar way. Trust me, that any attempt to reform the Church is like giving stimulants to a man far gone in a consumption. The patient very soon finds that the remedy is killing him outright. And this has been the case in a small way with the tonic which the wiseacres thought to administer to the convent of the Ursulines. I hear that the sisterhood are in a state of open rebellion;—that they are supported by some of the influential clergy of the diocese;—that there is likely to be such a row and a scandal as might even cause the existence of Montepulciano to be heard of in these latitudes. All which would be about as interesting to us as hearing that the Emperor of China had a cold in his head, were it not that it seems, from all I can hear, likely to lead to the new Abbess being summoned to Florence, and, as a consequence, to the recal of the Contessina Stella. You know my dear Uncle Florimond's diplomatic profundity and caution. Still, he is open to a certain amount of pumping, if the handle of the machine be not plied too roughly. And my impression is that he knows that it has been decided to bring the Contessina home. You must not suppose, however, that any such move is worth more than it really is. I have not the slightest hope that such a step would indicate any change in that terrible Canonico Adalberto's plans and purposes. There are plenty of other convents. But, at all events, it will give us an opportunity of communicating with the poor dear little exile; and that is worth something. Meanwhile, depend on me and the Palmieri to keep a sharp look out, to take advantage of any chance that may turn up, and to write directly if there is anything worth telling.

"So you have got your leave of absence at last. I congratulate you, and earnestly hope that your projected trip to Bologna may not turn out altogether fruitless for the object you have in view. I address this letter as usual, but suppose that it will, probably, have to follow you to Bologna.

"Yours always,

"CARLO."

To the above extracts from the letters of Carlo Brancacci it may be useful to add the following from Professor Pietro Varani to Giulio Malatesta, written just before the latter started on his long-deferred journey to Bologna, as it will serve to explain the objects and the prospects before Giulio with respect to the investigation he was bent on making:

"Most esteemed Signor Capitano,—

"I am much pleased to hear that you are at last able to accomplish your purpose of going to Bologna. You know, alas! too well, how much reason I have for feeling that the inquiries you intend making are—I will not say as deeply, for that would wrong the ardour of your filial feelings—but more painfully interesting to me than even to yourself. I dare not say to you or to myself that I have much hope. It is now nearly twenty-three years from the day, never to be forgotten by me, when my fatal ignorance and undue trustfulness in a scoundrel led to so much misery!—nearly twenty-three years!—a fatally sufficient time for effacing oblivion to do its work! To *me* every incident, every look of each of the actors in that sad scene, are as vividly present as they were while they were actually passing. But we cannot expect that such should be the case with others.

"I have called the worthless man who broke your dear mother's heart a scoundrel, and his subsequent conduct stamps him such; for it was in his power to make all right when it was discovered that the clandestine marriage was void, and he would not do so. But I have never supposed that he could have known the fatal flaw arising from my being under legal age before the marriage was made. I have told you this when we have talked the matter over together; and I have always come to the same conclusion in my many, many meditations on the subject.

"It would probably not be difficult to discover the house at which your mother resided at Belfiore, and perhaps the owners of it and others, who were about her at the time of her leaving it, might still be found. But I have little, or rather, I confess, no hope, that they will be able to throw any light on her destination, beyond its being Rome.

"I enclose you a letter to my mother, not so much from any hope that she can be of service to you by any recollection of her own—for she can scarcely know any of the facts, save such as were known to me—but simply because from her many years' residence in Bologna, and her long, close, and widely-extended connexion with the liberal party throughout Romagna, she may be able, perhaps, to be of use in making you acquainted with persons who may possibly be helpful to you. More especially, as at the present time it would scarcely be prudent for an officer in your service to be known as such in the Papal territory, she may be of use to you; for you may implicitly trust in that point of view any person with whom she may put you in relation.

"My mother is now a very old woman, and though when I last heard of her she was in somewhat failing health, is still in the full possession of all her faculties. You must not suffer yourself to be repulsed by any want of graciousness you may find in her manner of receiving you. She is an upright woman and means well, and will, I am sure, be willing to serve you in any way she can. But she is harsh and austere in manner. She has seen much of the wrong, the tyranny, and the abuses which, during the whole of a long life, have made her country one of the most wretched on the face of the earth. Her whole life has been spent in fighting against the laws and the makers of them, by force or by fraud, or by any available means. And she is, in consequence, a soured and embittered woman; and her tongue is apt to be sarcastic and mordant. Nevertheless, when she knows who and what you are, I am sure that she will wish to lend you a helping hand if she can; and, at all events, you may perfectly trust her.

"And so, my most valued friend, with heartfelt wishes for a successful result to your pilgrimage, I remain,

"Your devoted servant and sincere well-wisher,

"PIETRO VARANI, Professore."

The above letters all reached Captain Malatesta at Alessandria, where his regiment was quartered; for, owing to new and unexpected delays, he was not able to get away from his military duties till the first days of 1851.

It was on the 6th of January that he reached Bologna.

CHAPTER II.

MARTA VARANI.

THE years which bring a young man from nineteen to twenty-two or so, and which were near about those that had passed over Giulio Malatesta since we parted from him on the field of Curtatone, produce for the most part a greater change in a young man on the southern side of the Alps than in our less forcing climate. The ripening process goes on more rapidly as regards manhood, as well as other growths, under an Italian sun. But the change which any friend who had not seen him during the interval would have remarked in Giulio, was attributable only in part to the mere lapse of time. It was a change undoubtedly for the better; and it may be assumed as certain that Stella, being thoroughly in love with him, would have at once felt and declared as much. But it is, perhaps, not quite equally certain that, had she not been already in love with him, she would have been as powerfully attracted by his present appearance as she had been by that which she had so enthusiastically described to the Abbess at Montepulciano. That "most beautiful hair in the world," instead of floating in long curly locks from his temples, was cropped short. The pale and almost sallow cheek had become somewhat bronzed, and perhaps a little filled out. Those eyes, the versatility of whose expression Stella had so lovingly celebrated, had far less of dreamy reverie in them than of yore, and seemed to have altogether forgotten the "beseeching" mood, which had spoken so powerfully to her heart, in favour of the stern and commanding expression, which she had sometimes seen in them. But then, the versatile eyes might probably change their mood again, if they got a chance of again communing with those which had marked them in their "beseeching" aspect.

The entire man, however, could never again reassume the expression of three years ago. For the change which had taken place in him was mainly a moral change. It was not only that the dreamy student had become a captain of Lancers —though that metamorphosis involved a very considerable change in the inner as well as in the outer man—but that the social waif aimlessly floating down the stream towards an uncertain future, had become a citizen, with his place marked and allowed in the social system, with a career and its hopes, aims, duties, and ambitions open before him.

The change, as has been said, was altogether a favourable one; and Stella would have felt it to be so. For though the captain of Lancers certainly looked less poetical than the dreamy, long-haired student, Stella's *beau ideal* would instantly on seeing him have been changed from the image of a poet meditating the generation of mankind by the instrumentality of a regenerated Church, to that of a general of division successfully labouring to secure his country's place among the nations.

For love laughs at consistencies as well as at locksmiths.

Giulio's first care on arriving in Bologna was to send a messenger from his inn with the Professor's letter to his mother, and a request that Signora Varani would name an hour when he might call upon her. In fact, he knew no other means of taking the first step in the matter he was engaged in. He had never been in Bologna before, and had not a single acquaintance in the city. He wished to hear from Signora Varani's own mouth her reminiscences of the circumstances attending the clandestine marriage. But the principal service he expected from her, was an introduction to some person he could depend on for assistance in certain inquiries he was bent on making at Belfiore and at Fermo.

It was nightfall before the messenger returned with a word to say that La Signora Varani would be glad to see the gentleman at ten o'clock the next morning. And at that hour, guided by a boy sent from his inn, Giulio found himself in the quiet little *piazza* of San Domenico, and at the door of the old house in the corner opposite to the entrance of the church.

The lapse of all but a quarter of a century had produced no shadow of change in the sleepy, quiet little *piazza*, with its tall, deathly dull houses, its picturesque, irregular-shaped church, its curious, mediæval sarcophagus tombs, its grass-grown pavement, and its one or two silent Domenican monks sauntering about the cloister entrance, or sunning themselves under the southern wall of the nave. The grass-blades between the paving-stones and the black and white monks in the sunshine, might have been the self-same grass and men that were idly and uselessly running to seed and fading in the same places a quarter of a century ago. Italy had been played for and lost in the interval, the great political carnival had taken place, and the political masking had begun and ended in the interval, national hope had blazed up high, and had sunk again in dull glowing embers of suppressed fire in the interval; but the sleepy little *piazza* of San Domenico had never waked up, and was still slumberously basking in its sunshine as it did when Cesare Malatesta used to watch for Maddalena Tacca behind the deep shadow of the Foscherari tomb, three-and-twenty years ago.

Inside the old apartment on one side of the third-floor landing-place there was as little change in all save the inhabitants of it. There the change was considerable. The duties of his career had taken the Professor—the awkward, silent, absent student of a quarter of a century ago—to a distant city; and when his young sister, who had grown up to be the solitary sunbeam that shed any light of grace or gladness on the dull life of that dreary household, had elected to accompany her brother to his new home, their mother had made no objection, and had not appeared in any way to regret the arrangement. There had never been any great sympathy between the ungainly, ill-favoured, dreamy lad and his still handsome, active, practical, hard-natured mother. But it might have been supposed that it would have cost the mother a pang to part with the child of her age, the one bright thing near or belonging to her. Such did not seem to have been the case, however. The stern old woman set her face to walk forwards into the desert of a solitary old age, apparently quite contented to be left to finish her pilgrimage alone. Alone with the political friends and the political schemes, that is to say, which had made the business and the interest of her life, and which, indeed, made the little apartment on the third floor scarcely a desirable residence for a young girl just blooming into great beauty.

For, truth to say, the pursuits of Signora Varani's life, and the position she held among the more advanced (*i. e.* the more violent and active) section of the liberal party, brought her into contact, and made her obscure little home the house of call for men of very various sorts, and many among them not of the most desirable kind for the intimacy of a young girl. Old Marta Varani knew *all* the leading "patriots" of Bologna and Romagna, and among them no small number of men of the loftiest character, the most exalted views, and the highest culture. But when breaking the laws, and conspiring against the makers and the agents of them, is the business of a lifetime, the habits of such a lifetime, however admirable, however necessary, and however holy the resistance to the tyranny to be overturned may be, is sure to bring the habitual rebel and conspirator into relation with many persons of whom none of those good things can be said. The result is an evil, which spreads and ramifies itself widely and profoundly through all the body of the social system, and forms one item to be added to the long bill against a bad government.

Old Marta Varani was herself much changed. It was of course that she should be so; she was now nearly seventy years old. But she was more altered than she might have been. Yet, in some respects, she was the same. The tall, spare, rigid figure was as upright as ever; but she steadied her steps with a stout cane, and the hand which grasped it trembled a little as it did its office. The great dark eye was as flashing and as bright as ever, and the heavy bushy brow above it as strongly marked and as menacing as ever, but it was iron-grey instead of black; and the hair, as abundant as ever, lay in considerable disorder as of yore, in large iron-grey instead of raven-black masses on the temples and forehead, square and massive as ever, but yellow now instead of white, as they still had been twenty years ago. The yellow tint, indeed, of the entire face, and the shrunken appearance of the lower portion of it, which made it seem scarcely half its former size, and gave the great fierce eyes the look of being disproportionately large for the other features, were the worst of the marks that time had left, for they seemed to indicate ill health as well as old age.

Despite, however, all such warnings that her course was nearly run, old Marta Varani was as keenly intent and as busily occupied as ever on the interests and the hopes that had made the business of her life. For a period—just the few years during which the masking of the political Carnival had lasted—the business of conspiring and rebelling and hatching plots had been slack, and the conspirators' house of call had been in a great measure deserted. But when the masking was over, and the Pope was himself again, the trade became brisker than ever. Never, indeed, at the worst of times, had the tyranny and cruelty of the ecclesiastical government been more intolerable than during the years which immediately followed the dissipation of the delusion of a liberal Pope and Papacy. The old agents of the priestly despotism, who had been outraged, terrified, and furiously enraged by the mock liberalism of the political Carnival-time, which had banished them into holes and corners in every part of the Pontifical territory, crawled forth again eager to avenge themselves for their past mortification on the unfortunates who had been deluded by the Papal masking into committing themselves to the liberalising government of the last three years. Never did persecution rage so fiercely, so relentlessly. Never had the sportsmen of the ecclesiastical government so magnificent a battue as when the political covers had been filled by the trick that had thus deluded the unfortunate subjects of Pope-land.

The natural result was, that secret associations, conspiracies, and plots of all kinds, were once again as rife as ever, and old Marta Varani was once more in her element; and the dark stairs of the old house in the Piazza di San Domenico were again climbed at all sorts of strange hours by all sorts of strange visitors.

Malatesta was admitted by a girl, whom the old woman had found herself compelled by her infirmities to take as a servant. She had done so very reluctantly, for she wanted no eyes save her own to note the comings and goings in her house.

"Take a seat, Captain Giulio Malatesta," said the old woman, looking at him keenly from under her heavy brows, "and excuse me for not rising to receive you. I do not get up when I am once seated so readily as I used to. So! I see by my son's letter that you were at Curtatone,—on the right side, for a wonder, considering the name you bear. Italy has little reason, and old Marta Varani has as little, to love the name of Malatesta."

"It may be that Italy will hereafter feel and speak differently of the name, Signora. I know that my name must be especially distasteful to you."

"Humph! I have been told that you did good service at Curtatone, Signor Capitano; and doubtless Italy will hold it in remembrance—in better remembrance, it is to be hoped, than it will hold certain other deeds that have been connected with the name."

"And for yourself, Signora?" pleaded Giulio, with a deprecatory smile.

"For myself—it is possible that I might do the same—if it mattered to anybody what a poor lonely old woman thought on that or any other subject. Though my recollections of the name are, as you say, not pleasing ones."

"You allude, Signora, I cannot affect to doubt, to the unhappy circumstances attending the marriage of my parents?"

"Ay! My son's letter tells me the errand you have come hither on. What can I do to undo the mischief that he was gaby enough to allow to be wrought?"

"Nay, Signora, the mischief that was done that day can never be undone." The old woman shot a sharp glance at him from under her eyebrows as he said the words, and continued to scrutinise his face earnestly as he continued: "I had no thought of undoing it, but simply of endeavouring to discover some traces of the unfortunate mother whom I have never known."

"And my son seems to imagine that I can assist that object. But he never had common sense enough to eat his own soup without scalding his mouth! It was an unhappy business, that marriage! Your unfortunate mother was shamefully, scandalously deceived and betrayed. And my great gaby of a son, of course, with the best possible intentions, like all the rest of the fools who make most of the trouble in this world, must needs give his help to the job."

"It would have been very difficult for him, under the circumstances of the case, as I have heard them from him, to refuse to act as a witness."

"He always said that that vile animal, the Marchese Malatesta there at Fermo, had no previous knowledge that Pietro was under age, and that the marriage was, therefore, a nullity. He won't believe that it was intended from the first that the marriage should be void. He thinks, the simpleton! that such wickedness is too monstrous to be attributed to any man. As if all the history of our lives, and all the history of the lives of our forefathers, had any other teaching in them than this—that no imaginable atrocity, cruelty, treachery, baseness, practised by the privileged classes on the slaves who endure their yoke, can be either a matter of surprise to the victims, or a weight on the conscience of their tyrants!"

And the old woman raised aloft the staff in her feeble hand with a gesture of impotent indignation as she spoke, and a gleam flashed from her eye which might have fitted her for the representative of a sibyl in the act of inspired denunciation.

"Is it, then, your own persuasion, Signora, that the fact was otherwise than as my friend the Professor thinks—that the Marchese plotted the false semblance of a marriage, and was aware both of the fact that your son was under age, and of the nullity of the marriage that would follow from it?" asked Giulio, calmly and observantly attentive to gather any facts which might possibly serve to help him in his quest.

"Is it my persuasion? Assuredly it is! My son's age was a matter of notoriety to all the town. All his comrades knew it. It was not as if he had been a student from a distance. We are Bologna people. He had lived here all his life. I firmly believe that it was deliberately planned to provide for the nullity of the marriage."

"If I could only acquire a conviction that such was the case!" said Giulio, between his ground teeth.

"Why, what then? Even if it were not so—if

the man were not guilty in intention before the marriage, he was afterwards. Why did he not marry his victim when the nullity of the marriage was discovered?"

"The refusal to do so was bad enough," replied Giulio, frowning heavily; "but not so base beyond all precedent of baseness, as the preconcerted treachery which you attribute to him. Weakness, criminal and contemptible enough if you will—want of courage to resist the threats and importunities of his family may—not palliate but—explain the latter conduct. The former would imply an excess of vileness beyond all example, and I confess, to my mind, almost beyond credibility."

"The excess of vileness in an aristocrat which is beyond credibility, occupies a smaller and smaller space in the imagination as one grows older in this part of the world, Signor Capitano. By the time one has reached seventy, the mind refuses to conceive any such idea at all. Remember that the Marchese Cesare Malatesta knew perfectly well that his hand was promised to—a female of his own species. The courage needed to fly in the face of all those long-standing family arrangements, and upset them all by making a marriage with a nobody, would have been surely as great as any that could have been needed to resist the pressure of his family afterwards! No! no! The vile traitor knew what he was about from the beginning! I have no doubt on the matter! And my wise and sharp son was clever enough to lend his aid to a scheme which he would freely have sacrificed his life to prevent! Ay, that he would, freely. For he was very fond of her who became your mother."

"Was it so, really? Poor mother! And Pietro Varani, let me tell you, Signora, has one of the largest, noblest hearts that ever beat in a man's bosom!" And Giulio's voice trembled a little with emotion as he said it.

"Well, yes! I suppose he had," said the old woman, coolly; "but then it was shut up out of sight inside him. What one saw outside did not seem so noble. And then poor Pietro was always a fool."

"He is not a fool!" said Giulio, sternly and almost fiercely.

"Well, if you are content with his wisdom in the matter, I suppose I may be!" said old Marta, with an approach to a sneer.

"With all that he did, and meant to do, I am content. You think he was attached to my mother?" he added, after a pause.

"He was 'attached to her,' as you phrase it. He was so wise as to love her well enough to have given his life to secure her happiness with another man—the great, ugly, poor-spirited oaf!" said his mother, with bitterness, and a strange mixture of feelings at her heart; "and she lovely enough to have won the love of the loveliest! It needed a different sort of creature to snare her heart, I trow!"

"You must have been a very beautiful woman in your time, Signora Varani!" said Giulio, unceremoniously, looking at the old woman speculatively, and speaking the thoughts which his observation of her and her words generated in him, rather to himself than to her.

"I was so!" said the old woman, with a grim smile; "and, accordingly, I too——tasted the sweets and the bitterness thereof. Both flavours have passed away!"

"Ay! but it happens, sometimes, that the latter flavour remains in the mouth many a long year after the first has gone for ever!" said Giulio.

"How so?" returned the old woman, sharply, with a fierce flash from her eyes, and a scowl on her heavy brow. "What is your meaning, Signor Capitano? If you have any, speak it out at once, and plainly."

"Is it not too plain that it is so?" returned Giulio, calmly, and surprised at the old woman's manner. "What has been the case with my unfortunate mother? Do you think the bitterness is not still present with her, if, indeed, she is still living to suffer?"

"In the case of your mother?" said Signora Varani, more quietly; "yes, doubtless it is so! She has been very unfortunate, and the bitterness of her fate, if I am to judge by my son's letter, has not ceased with her, even if she herself has escaped from it."

"As regards myself, you mean, Signora?" rejoined Giulio. "Nay, my position in that respect weighs less heavily on me than you might imagine. Unless, indeed——" he added hastily, as the thought of the influence his birth might exercise on his hopes of Stella dashed across his mind; but he checked himself suddenly, and continued: "In truth, it irks me but little not to have been born the heir to a Marquisate. The days are at hand, nay, they have come, when it imports more to an Italian man what he is, than what his father was. I have made some steps towards finding for myself a place in the world which suits me better than that which would have been mine had the union of my parents been a legitimate one. And I am not afraid of the prospect before me as regards treading the remainder of the path. No! believe me, Signora, the sole thought that has brought me hither and urged me to my present quest, is the desire to know my mother, and the hope of alleviating her sorrows."

"And you do not burn with any noble ambition to be Marchese Malatesta and heir to all the Malatesta wealth, even if it were within your reach?" said Marta, looking fixedly at him.

"Pooh! pooh!" said he, smiling. "How should I ever have thought of what is as much out of my reach as it would be to be the Emperor of Russia? But, honestly, I have no more regret in not being one of those great potentates than the other. If you won't think me too great a coxcomb, I don't mind admitting, Signora, that I prefer, on the whole, being Captain Giulio Malatesta, of the Lancers, in his Piedmontese Majesty's service!"

"Unless, indeed——as you were saying just now, Signor Capitano?"

"Well, I stopped short in what I had been about to say, Signora, because I doubted whether I should like to go on!" said Malatesta, laughing; "but to the mother of my friend Pietro I do not mind acknowledging," he continued, with a bright blush, "that the circumstances of my birth would be felt as a calamity by me, if they should exercise a disastrous influence on my hopes of winning the hand of a certain fair lady."

"I suppose you have done the other part of the winning?" said the old woman, speaking more kindly to him than she had done hitherto.

"I have reason to hope that her heart is mine," said Giulio.

"And would it be encroaching too far on your confidence to ask who the fair lady may be?" asked the old woman, with a very grim smile, which was intended to be a very kind one. "Look you here, Signor Capitano," she went on, before he had time to answer her, "I don't like many people, and specially I am not apt to take a liking to new faces, however good-looking they may be, the first time of seeing them. But I *do* like a man who has no desire to become Marchese Malatesta, and who would rather make his own place in the world than find it ready made for him. And it may be—it is possible that it might be—that I could lend you a helping hand in one way or another. There are more folks in the world, and in all sorts of queer corners of it, who would do a turn for poor old Marta Varani, than you would think for."

"Thanks for your kind opinion, Signora. What you ask is no secret. The lady in question is the Contessina Stella Altamari of Florence. And strangely enough, I learn by her letters, that since I have left Florence her family have proposed to her, and attempted to compel her to marry—of all people in the world that the malice of Fortune could have selected—the Marchesino Alfonso Malatesta of Fermo!"

"Your father's legitimate son and heir!" exclaimed the old woman—"your half-brother! By all the saints, it is a queer turn of Fortune's wheel! And what sort of a gentleman may this Marchesino be?"

"I know nothing of him—never saw him—scarcely ever heard of him. It is enough that Stella has no liking for him—would have no liking for him, even if he had not been forced on her as a pretender to her hand."

"And how came such a proposal to be made?" asked Signora Varani.

"It was the doing of an uncle of the Contessina Stella's, it seems—a certain Canonico Altamari. He is bent on uniting two large properties together."

"So the Canonico Altamari is bent on marrying his niece. Has the lady father or mother?"

"Neither, Signora; she lives with an aunt, the Contessa Zenobia Altamari."

"And the priest uncle is bent on marrying his niece to the Malatesta Marquisate, and the Malatesta estates?"

"That is the state of the case."

"And the Lady Stella prefers the illegitimate son, who fought at Curtatone, and is captain of Lancers, with no estates at all, to the legitimate Marquis, who is a faithful son of Mother Church, and who has all that such a legitimate Marquis and faithful son should have, eh?"

"That also is, I believe, the state of the case," answered Giulio, smiling at the odd manner of the old lady.

"Humph!" she said, placing both hands on the handle of her stick, and leaning her forehead upon them in front of her chair.

"Look you, Signor Capitano," she resumed, after a pause, as she raised her head to look at him, "you shall do me the pleasure of leaving me for half an hour, for I want to think. Go and take a turn in the cloisters of the church over there; it is a pleasant sunny place enough—it was there your poor mother used to walk and listen to the words of the noble gentleman who deceived her—and come back to me in half an hour. I want to think of a thing or two."

Giulio, not a little surprised, and somewhat amused at the strangeness of the old woman's whims, did as he was bid; and for want of any better mode of occupying the prescribed half-hour, adopted her suggestion of spending it in the Dominican cloister.

It seemed that the old woman's blunt request had expressed her purpose simply and truly. For as soon as the door had closed behind her guest, she remained awhile apparently plunged in absorbing meditation.

"Ha, ha, ha! ho, ho, ho!" she laughed suddenly,

with as much bitterness as merriment in her tone. "I swear by all the saints it would be worth doing, if it were only for the fun of it! What a cawing and fluttering there would be in the rookery! It don't come easy, though, after so long," she muttered to herself, after a pause; "and yet what should I care for now," she continued, musingly; "I did care once! I had my whistle, and paid for it! I didn't think it would ever cost so dear, though! And now the play is over—very nearly over, as far as I have any part to play in it—very nearly over! And what do I care what they say! I wonder how I ever came to care so much as I did! For I *did* care! 'You must have been a handsome woman,' said the young Captain! There were others found that out before him. I suppose one cares more for what the world says, when one is fed on its admiration and praise! And then, when the thing was done, it was terribly difficult to undo it again. There's lots of other things like that! And then Pietro? What about Pietro? The largest and noblest heart, said the stranger, that ever was in a man's bosom. He's not far out, the stranger! I wonder how it was that Pietro and I were never closer to each other. I wish he had been a good-looking lad! And yet it was for his sake——No! that's a lie, Marta Varani! It was for your own sake. And now, when your share of the game is over, you'll make your snivelling confession, and leave the shame of it to him. And yet—I wonder what Pietro would say, if he were asked! Don't I know that's a lie again, to pretend to have any doubt what he would say! Let right be done, he would say! No mistake about that! The largest heart in that ugly misshapen carcase of his! The Captain there could find that out, though that pretty fool, Maddalena Tacca, could not. The largest and noblest heart, said he. My notion is, that his own is not one of the smallest or least noble! I like that Captain Malatesta. He is handsome outside as well as in. I wish I could have had such a son as he! Well, well! I have nearly done with wishing at this time of day! Poor Pietro! how would it be to him? The Captain there has one misfortune; he is on the sunny side of the world's hedge, all but in that respect. He is brave, handsome, beloved by the girl he loves, stands well with his fellows and friends! He is all right, save for the one blot. And *my* son, poor Pietro! How much of the world's sunshine has he had? And now to take the one blot out of the Captain's lot and transfer it to his! To say to him, 'This bright and happy fellow, your friend here, has got only one little burden laid on his shoulder by fate. You have such a fardel that it can't make much difference to you to carry his for him also!' That is what I must say to

Pietro. Ay! but *is* it his and not Pietro's? Justice! Pshaw! When is there justice in this world! It would be very hard on poor Pietro. Poor Pietro, who has so little of good on this earth! No, Marta Varani, that is not it! You are lying again. I *will* tell the truth to myself, whoever else I may lie to! It was for myself and not for him that I did it; and it is for myself and not for him, that I am now afraid of undoing it. What would it matter to him, the Professor at Pisa! Not the difference of a fig's end! What would it matter to the handsome young Captain there? Everything! Give him his wife! no doubt about that! Find him his mother! For the old scoundrel at Fermo would have to speak out then, and if the poor soul is above ground we should soon find her. Give the scoundrel Marchese his due! Make the aristocrats eat such dirt, that it would be a treat to see them at it! Secure the wealth to the good cause! And what stands in the way of all that? Only I! Not Pietro; only I. How to stand up against the scorn and the opprobrium, and the reprobation for not having spoken during these years! That is the point! It can't be for long; that's one thing. The play is nearly played out for me. If it were only quite played out! If I could be sure the end was close at hand! Wait till then? Speak my secret, and then be off without waiting to hear what any one may have to say about it! I do not think the end is far off; and I am sure I am tired enough! If I wait awhile, till I am sure of my escape? Ay! but waiting may spoil all for him."

At this point of the meditations, represented by the above phrases as accurately as the unspoken working of the mind can be translated into words, the old woman was interrupted by the return of Giulio from his half-hour's banishment. Her first thought on his return was that she had not half done thinking yet—that she needed more time for coming to some decision on the doubts which had been the subject of her pondering.

"The half-hour is gone, is it?" she said; "I thought I had not been alone half that time! But now, young sir, I will tell you what I recommend in the first instance. I can give the name and address of the people with whom your mother lodged at Belfiore, near Foligno. Go there, and ascertain if they can furnish you with any information, or any clue. It is possible; and you would not be satisfied without having made the attempt. And when you have done this, whether with any success or not, come back here to me. I do not despair of being able to help you. Come back, do you hear, in any case, whether you learn anything at Belfiore or not. Do not take any further step without first coming back to me. Do you agree to that?"

"I will do so, Signora, in any case; and feel truly grateful for your readiness to assist me," said Giulio.

"Ah! truly grateful! And will you continue truly grateful to old Marta Varani, if I *should* succeed in finding your mother for you?"

"I trust so, Signora! Surely I should, to the end of my days."

"To the end of my days would be enough! Well, perhaps, we shall see! Now I will get you the address at Belfiore."

And the old woman, after a little searching in a cabinet containing a quantity of papers, took out an old yellow letter, which had been written to Pietro by the woman with whom Maddalena had lodged at Belfiore, after her departure thence. From this she made him copy the name and address, and dismissed him.

The next morning Giulio started for Foligno.

CHAPTER III.

THE SEALED PACKET.

It will not be necessary to follow Captain Malatesta in his expedition to Belfiore. It was tedious, disappointing, and finally fruitless. His first inquiries at the little village were met by the information, that the owner of the house in which his mother had lived more than twenty years ago had died shortly after that time; that his widow had married again, and was now living at Viterbò. He went thither, and after some little difficulty found out the person he was in quest of, only to be told that, though remembering all the circumstances to which he referred perfectly well, she was unable to afford him any information on the point in question. The poor lady had gone away, apparently willingly, with the gentleman who had come from Rome, and who had represented himself as about to return thither immediately. But a maid-servant, who had been living in the house at Belfiore at the time, had been just about to visit her relatives at Foligno at the time of the gentleman's arrival from Rome. And he had kindly permitted her to avail herself, on his return, of his carriage for the little journey from Belfiore to that city. She had sat in the carriage with the two travellers during the hour or so which that short drive would occupy. It was very possible, therefore, that she might have become acquainted with their plans when they should have arrived at Rome. This woman was still living at Belfiore. It was worth while to speak with her; especially as the little village at the foot of the Apennine was very little out of the road by which Giulio must needs return to Bologna.

He went back again therefore to Belfiore;—to be again disappointed. The person in question remembered well her little journey to Foligno with the poor lady and the strange gentleman in black. But all she could report was, that the lady was weeping during the whole time, and no word whatever passed between her and the gentleman.

There appeared no further chance of obtaining at Belfiore any clue to the information he was in search of. Nevertheless, Giulio did not regret his journey thither. He had no difficulty in meeting with many persons who remembered the circumstances of his mother's residence in the village. Specially one, a daughter of the family in which she had lived, who must have been a year or so younger than Maddalena Tacca, and who was at the time of Giulio's visit living in the village, the mother of children now nearly of the same age, had apparently been her frequent companion, remembered her still with interest, and was well pleased to talk with Giulio by the hour together of his mother and of her habits and mode of life while at Belfiore.

Susanna Biraggi—that was the married name of Maddalena's former companion—told at length how happy in each other the handsome young couple had appeared when they first came there. She related how letters had arrived which were as the first gathering clouds of the storm, that so soon wrecked that summer-tide happiness. She described the growing paleness of the young bride's cheek, and growing alienation of the man on whose affection her life-springs depended. She told the story of his departure; of the lingering hope, which would not be killed, that he would return; of the letters from Fermo, and the terrible despair which followed them. She showed Giulio the favourite walk beneath the poplars by the side of the little stream, where it issues from its ravine in the Apennine, where his mother used to take her solitary walk, and the stone bench under the roadside Madonna, where day after day, with ever renascent hope, she would await the coming of the postman from Foligno.

And all these reminiscences were inexpressibly valuable to Giulio. He led his new acquaintance again and again to describe to him the regular-featured, oval-visaged, delicate-complexioned beauty of his mother's face, and the tall, slender figure, so elastic in its springy gait at first, so sadly drooping in the latter part of her residence among the villagers. And he felt, as he listened to all this, and fed his fancy with the images supplied by the associations attached to the localities, as if the individuality of his unknown mother was assuming a consistency in his imagination, which made it possible for her to become the object of a more personal and less merely theoretic love than he had before been capable of feeling for her. But it was with a passionate emotion, strangely composed of sweet and bitter feelings, that he heard Signora Biraggi tell how the deserted wife's consciousness that she was about to become a mother, had, contrary to Nature's sweet provision, been turned to sorrow, and dread, and agony. And oh! how eagerly he longed that it might yet be possible for him to restore the joy of motherhood to that poor tortured heart, and teach the victim even yet to thank God that she had brought a child into the world.

Giulio returned from Belfiore to Bologna without having made the smallest step in advance towards the discovery of his mother. But he did not regret his journey, nor the fortnight it had cost him; for the reminiscences of her which he had gathered were very precious to him.

On his return to Bologna, he found the letter from Stella, which has been given in a former chapter, awaiting him at the post-office; and at his hotel a note written by a stranger on behalf of Signora Varani, urgently requesting him to lose no time in coming to her. The language of the latter was so pressing, that he would not have delayed even the few minutes necessary to read the letter he had just received at the post-office, had it been written in any other hand. But it was impossible to put off reading Stella's epistle. He ran over it, therefore, hastily; and putting it in his pocket for reperusal at his first leisure moment, hurried off to the Piazza di San Domenico, anxiously weighing in his mind, as he walked, the probable value of the mysterious hints in Stella's strange communication.

The door of Signora Varani's apartment was

opened to him by a stranger, who was, however, evidently aware that he was expected.

"You are, I presume, the Signor Capitano Malatesta?" said the stranger. "You have come in time; and that is about as much as can be said. The Signora Marta cannot last many hours. She has been very anxious for your coming. I am Onesimo Badaloni, doctor of medicine, at your service."

"Not last many hours! Her illness has been very sudden, then? Can I see her now directly? What has been the nature of her malady?"

"Mainly old age!" replied the physician. "She has lived her time, and is worn out, that is all. There have been slight symptoms of paralysis of the heart, which in her case is likely enough to have been brought on by any unusual excitement or emotion. But, *che vuole!* At seventy years of age these things are occasions but not causes!—Yes, you can see her at once. She is perfectly herself, and has been anxiously asking for you—wanting to send to the hotel, to see if you had returned, every half-hour. Come in, Signore. I will just tell her you are here."

In half a minute Doctor Badaloni returned from the inner room, saying that the dying woman begged Captain Malatesta to come to her immediately.

As he entered the room, he met the gaze of the

old woman, as she sat propped up in bed, looking eagerly towards the door. Her face seemed yet more shrunken and fallen than before; and her breath appeared to come short, and with some little difficulty. But there were the great black eyes, flaming out more brightly and fiercely than ever, Giulio thought, from the yellow, desiccated parchment-looking face.

"So you have come at last! Well for you that you did not delay a little longer; for I should not have waited for you, I can tell you! Now have the kindness, Signor Capitano, to see if the doctor has left the house, and if the door is shut after him; and call the girl out of the kitchen to me. You are not to open the door," she said to the girl, "to any one while this gentleman is with me, do you understand? And you are to stay in the kitchen yourself, and shut the door, do you hear? And do you close the door of this room after her, Signor Capitano! So! now I can say what I have to say to one pair of ears only. Stop a minute!"

After lying back on the pillow for a few instants, with her eyes closed to rally her failing strength, she continued:

"It is not an easy matter to say what I have to say even to one hearer, you see; and therefore I have no wish for more. Again and again I have been tempted to wish that you might not come back in time, and then I should have died and kept my secret; and it would not have been my fault. But you are in luck! and in good time. I suppose," she added, after another pause of a minute or so, "that you did not succeed in getting any information at Belfiore?"

"No! Signora Varani! I met with people who remembered my poor mother well, and who could tell me many things about her, but nothing to furnish any clue to her present retreat. On my return to this city, however, I found a letter from the young lady I mentioned to you the other day, holding out the hope that the Superior of the convent in which she has been placed, may be able to give me the information I am in search of. It would seem from her letter as if she were herself in possession of more definite information, but were, for some reason or other, forbidden to speak more clearly."

"Where is the convent in which the young lady is residing?" asked Signora Varani.

"At Montepulciano;—a convent of Ursulines," replied Giulio.

"The most likely thing for them to have done with her was to bury her in a convent, poor thing!" returned the old woman; "and it is probable enough that the Superior may know something of her. Those people always keep up a correspondence between one house and another of the same order. What shall you do?"

"I must go and speak with this Abbess," said Giulio; "it is what Stella's letter invites me to do."

"Ah! but you must first do what I am going to invite you to do. When you have done that, you will find your mother safe enough,—if she is still alive. You told me the other day, Signor Capitano, that I must have been a beautiful woman in my day. Well, I was so! There were few girls in Bologna more thought of than I was, when I was in my prime. I was no worse than your mother was, Signor Capitano, and she was a great beauty. Well! the flies come round the sugar now-a-days; and they did just the same half a century ago! What happened to your mother, happened to me. Not quite the same, though, to be honest; I knew what I was doing, and she did not. In another way, however, the difference was in my favour. The man I loved was worthy of a woman's love. He became my husband—as soon as circumstances made it convenient for him to do so."

The dying woman lay back on the pillows gasping with the effort it had cost her to speak the above sentences. Giulio offered her a glass of water, but she put his hand away, and remained perfectly still, but for the laborious heaving of her chest, for several minutes.

"Now give me a drink of water," she said, at the end of that time. "There, that will do," she continued; "I am not dead yet. I have time enough for what remains to be said. Pietro little thought, when he sent you to me, what I could do for you! Tell him so; tell him that I sacrificed the object of a lifetime, and spent my last breath in doing it, because I knew that if he were here it is what he would wish me to do. Now take this paper," she continued, drawing a sealed packet from beneath the pillows under her head. I prepared this after you were gone, as soon as I saw that my end was at hand. But I am not sure that I should not have destroyed it, if you had not come back in time. Take it! There is a statement in it made before a notary, and witnessed by him. Perhaps it was not necessary to make it. But what is more to the purpose, and would, I suppose, have sufficed without the other, there is the address of a place in the south of France to which you will have to go. Perhaps you may be short of money for such a journey. Take from that cabinet the rouleau you will see just inside the door. There are two hundred and fifty dollars. You will give all that you do not need to Pietro; and repay him afterwards whatever you use of it. You will find directions what you are to do; it is all clear enough—*pur troppo!**—and as

* "Only too clear!"

soon as you have the necessary papers you will come back here at once, and cause right to be done."

Here again she stopped, exhausted, and remained for several minutes with her eyes closed, and breathing heavily, while Giulio stood, with the packet in his hand, anxiously watching the flickering flame of the expiring life, and lost in astonishment at what he had heard.

"Perhaps," she said, after a time, "I may not be so near my end as I thought for. Maybe, I may live yet a day or two! I am sure I don't want to! I have had enough of it. But what I was going to say was this; and mind you obey me!" she added, with a momentary gleam of the old fire in her eyes: "You are not to open that packet till the breath is out of my body, do you hear? As soon as I am dead, but not before! Do you promise?"

"Certainly, Signora! The papers are yours!"

"Ay! and the secret is mine; mine, as long as the breath remains in my body. You promise?"

"I have promised, Signora! This packet shall not be opened by me till after your death."

"Very good! Now you may tell the girl that she may open the door, and let the priest come in when he arrives. The doctor said he would send him. Not that old Marta Varani wants any priest to help her to die! But they make such a bother, you see, that it is easiest to let them have their way! And now *addio*, Signor Capitano. I am glad my son sent you to me. When you know my secret, don't be hard upon me; and remember, that if I began by doing you an ill turn, I ended by doing you a very good one. *Addio!*"

"But I can't leave you in this way, *cara mia Signora*, alone with that girl! Pray allow me to remain with you——" said Giulio, feeling it to be impossible to abandon the dying old woman to the care of the young girl, who was the only living creature in the solitary habitation with her. But old Marta would not hear of his remaining.

"No! no! you must be off, and that quickly," she said, "for I have another matter still to settle before I die; and there will be a certain person here presently, who would not approve of the presence of a third, while he transacts his business. I have to give up into proper safe keeping papers that would hang and ruin half Bologna. He who is to take charge of them will be here directly. And don't suppose, young sir," she added, after a pause, "that old Marta Varani is left to die alone and unfriended like a dog in a ditch! I need but to hold up my finger to have the room full of watchers and friends. Ah! if you were a Romagnole, you would know that I might have half the best men in Romagna by my death-bed, if I chose it. *Addio*, Signor Capitano! If I die in the course of the night, you may be off on your journey to-morrow morning."

Thus dismissed, Giulio had no choice but to leave the old woman as she bade him.

"Farewell then, Signora! since it must be so," said Giulio, taking in his one of the withered hands that were lying on the counterpane of the bed; "I would I had any better means of expressing my gratitude for the interest you have taken in my affairs, than by merely saying I thank you. But I *am* grateful. May God bless you!"

"Wait, and see whether you will say as much when you know the secret. Do, if your heart will let you. *Addio!*"

As Giulio stepped out upon the still *piazza*, with no occupation before him in Bologna save to wait for the last sigh of the strange woman he had just left, he turned into the quiet cloister in which he had spent half an hour at the old woman's bidding on a former occasion, deeply musing on the strangeness of the scene he had just passed through, and on all the possibilities that occurred to him as an explanation of the secret which had been confided to him.

What was the meaning of the hints which the dying woman had let drop of a similarity between her fate and that of his mother? And this journey to France? What could that have to do with the discovery of his mother's place of retreat? Had Marta Varani the means of knowing that she was in France? And what could be the explanation of her anxiety that the secret, whatever it might be, should not be discovered till after her death?

He drew out the sealed envelope which had been given him, and gazed at it!—a cover of thick coarse paper, and a large seal, with the impress on it of a small coin! The packet was not large or heavy. There could be no great quantity of writing in it! And this was about all that could be deduced from looking at it.

Then he took from his pocket Stella's letter, and sat himself down on the slab beneath the red marble effigy of the ancient warrior, which marked the spot where his mother had so often listened to the false wooing that had lured her to her fate; and having first cast a sharp glance along the cloister right and left of him, to make sure that he was alone, as his father had done in the same spot of yore, he pressed the letter to his lips, and then proceeded to re-read it, slowly and deliberately, savouring every word of it. Of course the perusal was exquisitely delightful to him. Of course it gave him infinitely greater pleasure than any other composition, though it should have combined the most impassioned eloquence with the choicest treasures of imagination, could have done. But when he came to read for the third time, and ponder on those parts in which the mysterious hints were thrown out of the probability that a clue might be furnished him to the finding of his mother, and compare them with what he had been hearing from the mother of the Professor, he could make nothing of the mystery. The old woman, who was then dying in the neighbouring house, had strictly enjoined on him to go first on the errand on which she was sending him to France, before proceeding to see the Abbess at Montepulciano. Should he obey her in this respect? No undertaking to do so was included in the promise he had given her. The temptation that drew him towards Montepulciano was very strong. What connexion could there be, or rather could there be any connexion, between the hopes Signora Varani might have of tracing his mother by means of information to be sought in the south of France, and those which Stella held out of finding her by the help of the Superior of the Montepulciano convent?. And yet, again, Signora Varani, when he had told her of Stella's hints respecting the information to be derived from the Abbess, had seemed to think it probable that the desired clue might be found in that manner!

Possibly the opening of the packet would furnish him with the means of comprehending the matter, and coming to a decision respecting his movements, as soon as the old woman should be no more. Till that event, he was fully decided to remain in Bologna.

Before leaving that part of the city to return to his inn, he went up again to the door of Signora Varani's apartment, and inquired after her of the girl who opened the door. He was told that she seemed to be no worse, and that she was engaged in business with a gentleman who had come shortly after he, Giulio, had left the house. It was very possible, he thought to himself, that the old woman might live some days longer—on the cards, even, that she might so far recover as to live for years! And with these thoughts in his head, he sat down to write to Stella in answer to her letter, intending to enclose his to her in one to the Superior of the convent.

"Bologna, Jan. 29, 1851.

"I wonder, my own beloved, whether you can figure to yourself the delight your darling letter has given me. Of course you will say you can measure it by the pleasure these present lines will give you! But is it quite the same thing? You know pretty well, in a general way, what my life has been. You have had nothing to fear for me. You do not need to be told that my heart is as much—nay more, Stella, certainly more—your own, than when we parted at the *veglione*, at three o'clock on Shrove-Tuesday morning. I need that information, it is true, as little as you do; and yet it is very sweet to receive it too! But then, think of my anxiety to hear a voice from that voiceless grave in which they have buried you. Oh! my Stella, when I think that the dreary, dreary months of your imprisonment have been the penalty and the proof of your love, I have no words which can express to you my tenderness and gratitude. And when I reflect on the trouble and difficulties which may yet be before us, I almost feel as if I ought to repent me of the wrong I did you in telling you my love, and daring to ask for yours in return. It is no true repentance, however, I fear. For that, we are taught, implies such change of mind as would assuredly prevent us from repeating the sin. And, my Stella, no such repentance is mine! If the deed were to be done afresh, if that ever-memorable night were to be passed over again, with the trembling hopes and horrible fears of its earlier hours, and the intoxicating triumph and joy of its conclusion, I should again be guilty of the selfishness of seeking to unite your fate with mine! I cannot repent, my beloved, though my heart bleeds to think on what you have gone through; and my admiration for the heroism of your resistance admonishes me what the man ought to be who should be worthy of you.

"Of course you will have imagined all the wondering, and puzzling, and speculation which the latter part of your letter is causing me. You will see also, by the date of this, that it has been an extraordinary long time in reaching me. Why it should have been so I have no means of guessing. You excuse yourself for writing mysteriously, telling me that you are not permitted to speak more clearly. Will you believe that I am not revenging myself in kind when you shall read this letter, and find that I am about to write to you in precisely similar strain, with a precisely similar excuse. It is strange enough that two such perfectly unmysterious persons as you and I should find themselves obliged each to play the sphynx to the other!

"My riddle is as follows:

"You know with what object I have come to Bologna. You know enough of my poor mother's story to understand why it should seem possible that some clue to her place of concealment might be found in this city. You will, no doubt, remember, also, the unfortunate connexion between her miserable story and my excellent friend Professor Varani at Pisa. Well! he gave me a letter to his mother, a very strange old lady, living here all by herself, at seventy years of age, or near it. Some day I will describe to you at length her eccentric manner of receiving me. For the present, it will suffice to tell you of the upshot of my interviews with her. In the first place, she sent me off to Belfiore, a village near Foligno, where my mother lived immediately after her unhappy marriage. It was possible that tidings might be heard of her there, and I went. I did, indeed, succeed in gathering many reminiscences of her from those who recollected her, which were inexpressibly precious to me, but no shadow of information that could help me to discover her. I returned hither, and found in the first place your dear letter, my own love, infinitely dear, despite all its intelligibilities; for would it not be so, even if couched in hieroglyphics, so that it were only certain that your own darling little hand had traced them!

"But I found, also, a summons calling me in all haste to the bedside of Signora Varani, who had been taken suddenly ill during my absence, and who was, and is still, to all appearances, dying. Well, my Stella, after much very strange and entirely unintelligible talk, she handed me a sealed packet, making me promise solemnly not to open it till after her death, and at the same time telling me that she was rendering me a great service; that I must immediately after her death go to the south of France, to an address which I shall find within the packet, and that I shall, after that, have no difficulty in finding my mother! Was ever anything so inexplicably mysterious? It is possible that the opening of the packet may, in some degree, solve the mystery, for she spoke of "directions," and of a "statement." But it seems at least equally probable that the explanation may only be reached when I have made the journey she bids me. At all events, I have determined to obey her, and go to the place to which I am directed. I will not throw away the possibility of a chance. Moreover, the old lady laid much stress on her injunctions that I should make this journey before going to Montepulciano. For I told her all about the mysterious hopes held out in your letter. And although you may guess, my heart's treasure, how eager I am to respond to the invitation, which may possibly afford me a chance of seeing you, I shall nevertheless obey Signora Varani in this also. There was a strange manner about her which strongly impressed me with the idea that she knew more about the matter than she chose to tell me. And I think that if you had heard her, you would feel with me, that it would be foolish not to be guided by her direction in the matter.

"Here, then, my Stella, is my mystery; and I flatter myself that, mystery for mystery, it is as mysterious as yours. May the discovery I would give so much to make result from one or both of them!

"And now, my own, what shall I say to you of myself? I can make no pretence to bravery, constancy, and heroism such as yours, dearest! My life, since the great piece of good fortune which gave me my commission, has been a hum-drum and ordinary one enough, busied with the regular duties of my profession, but prosperous to a degree truly beyond my deserts. And my prospects for the future are good. I may say to you, my own love, that I stand well with my superiors, and look forward to my career with the confidence of doing something. The opportunity, moreover, will not be wanting; for, depend on it, Stella, Italy has not said her last word. Our recent heavy mischances have been a check, but not a final defeat. There will be, assuredly, work for Italian swords before long! And the upward path will be open to those who are minded to tread it.

"As to our mutual hopes for the future, what can I say? It would be too presumptuous in me to talk of firmness and courageous hope to you, who have shown so much of them. But I may speak my own conviction, that with patience we shall triumph over the obstacles in our way. Remember, when the members of your family talk of condemning you to the veil, that they cannot wish to see the Altamari property go away, as it in that case would, to a distant branch of the family. Would, my Stella, that it were all gone away, to the distant branch or anywhere else, so that it did not stand, as it does, in the way of our happiness!

"And now, dearest, I must bring this unconscionably long letter to an end. I am about to enclose it in one to your Superior, knowing well—*pur troppo!*—that that is the only means by which it can reach you. From your account of the Abbess, I presume that it has a fair chance of doing so through her. My letter to her will, of course, be merely to say that, in consequence of the messages which have reached me, I shall wait upon her at the earliest date my avocations will permit of my doing so.

"I must in any case remain here till all shall be over with the poor old Signora Varani. As soon as that is the case, and I am at liberty to break the seal of her packet, I shall write again.

"Your own

"GIULIO.

"P.S.—Tidings have reached me of certain differences in your ecclesiastical world of Montepulciano, which might eventually lead to the removal of your Abbess to Florence, and, as a consequence, to your own recal thither. I hardly know whether such an event would be desirable for us or not, under all the circumstances. But I do not hesitate to address this letter to Montepulciano. For if any such move had already taken place, I should not have been left by our friends in ignorance of it.

"Once again, my beloved one, now and ever,

"Your own

"GIULIO."

The letter to the Abbess, in which the foregoing was enclosed, ran as follows:

"REVEREND MOTHER,—

"I take the liberty of addressing your maternity in consequence of a communication received by me from the lady to whom the enclosed is addressed, and to whom, I trust, you will feel it to be consistent with your duty to deliver it. The letter from her, to which I refer, though bearing date some months since, only reached me at this city yesterday. The delay in replying to it, therefore, has been from no neglect of mine.

"It appears, from what the Lady Stella has written, that some conversations have passed between your maternity and her, from which certain particulars of my personal history have become known to you, and you have been made aware of my earnest wish and endeavour to find out the unfortunate mother from whom I was separated before I could have the blessing of knowing her. It would seem also, from what the Contessina Stella writes to me, that your maternity has reason to suppose that it might be possible for you to afford me information which might assist me in the search in which I am engaged; and that with so holy and charitable an object in view, you would have the kindness to admit me to speech with your maternity, if I would wait upon you at Montepulciano. Business here, connected with the same great object of my life, makes it impossible for me instantly to go to Montepulciano for this purpose; but your maternity may rely on my not failing to do so very shortly.

"With the most heartfelt thanks for the charity which has prompted your maternity to offer your assistance to a motherless son engaged in a quest which cannot but be deemed a holy and pious one,

"I am, of your maternity,

"The obedient and devoted son,

"Giulio Malatesta, Captain."

When Giulio had finished his writing, he proceeded to read over his letters, and was sufficiently well contented with the latter and shorter one, the composition of which had cost him some thought and study. But with his letter to his love, which had run from his pen as fast as his hand could write it, he was profoundly disgusted. It seemed utterly to fail in expressing his feelings—cold—flat—and jejune. He had nearly determined on tearing it up and beginning again, and was only deterred from doing so by the conviction that he should succeed no better. He at last, therefore, in very ill humour with his own capacities, contented himself with adding a second postscript, to the following effect:

"On reading over my letter to you, my Stella, I am disgusted at finding how totally it fails to tell you how——anything, in short, of all I long to tell you, and that it seems to me I could tell you, if I could have the ineffable delight of doing so. Perhaps, if I had that chance, I should not be more able to speak than I am to write! I am not good at either, my Stella. But though I cannot imitate the eloquence of your dear letters, which bring the tears into my eyes every time I read them, I can love! And I can only implore of you, my dear one, to believe that the heart may feel more than the unready tongue or the unpractised pen can succeed in expressing.—G. M."

It was late in the night before Giulio had completed, sealed, and addressed his letters. Early the next morning his first care was to post his packet, and his second to hurry to the Piazza di San Domenico. He met the medical man coming down the staircase, and learned from him that Signora Varani had rallied a little during the night; that it was very possible she might live yet a few days; but that he did not think it at all probable that her life would be prolonged beyond that time.

There was nothing for it, therefore, but for Giulio to resign himself, with such patience as he might, to awaiting the event in Bologna.

CHAPTER IV.

STELLA'S RETURN HOME.

On the first of March—about four weeks, that is to say, after the date of the letters given in the last chapter—a large packet arrived from Montepulciano at Florence, addressed, "To the Very Reverend and Illustrious Signor, the Signor Canonico Adalberto Altamari." It was sealed with the seal of the Chancery of the Diocese of Montepulciano, and it contained the two letters from Giulio to the Abbess and to Stella, together with another to the Canonico Altamari, couched in the following terms:

"Very Reverend Sir, and esteemed Brother in Christ,—

"Beyond all doubt, your reverence, placed as you are by Providence and by your illustrious rank in a position in the metropolis which enables you to observe and take note of the transactions of the Universal Church, will have had your attention called to the deplorable disorders and scandals which have vexed and are still likely further to afflict this poor diocese of Montepulciano. It is well known in high quarters, and therefore, of course, to your illustrious reverence, that the many Christian graces and admirable virtues which adorn the character of our estimable Bishop, and which, despite the adverse feeling of nearly every other dignitary in the diocese, have rendered him especially beloved and honoured by me, are, nevertheless, not of that kind which are needed for the judicious government and administration of a diocese in these difficult times. The result is, that very deplorable irregularities and scandals have arisen, to the great grief and perplexity of the more judicious, more zealous, and more right-minded members of the clergy; and that a larger portion of the duty of struggling against these, and finding remedies for them, has fallen on my humble shoulders than would have been the case in a diocese ruled by—I may venture to say in confidence to your illustrious reverence—a more competent Bishop. It is unquestionably true that the responsible and laborious position of Chancellor of this diocese, in which, after having laboured for a long course of years, I was suffered to remain at the death of our late Bishop, of blessed memory, to the surprise certainly, but God forbid that I should say *to the scandal of all the diocese*, renders it fitting that I should not shrink from the discharge of duties that, in a more fortunately-circumstanced church, would fall to the share of the Bishop. It is true, also, that the office of Director of the Convent, the internal government of which has brought it recently so disastrously before the Christian world, has been discharged by me, I think I may venture to say, in such a manner as to have secured the unvarying confidence and esteem of those holy sisters for very many years; and that this circumstance also makes it, in a great measure, incumbent upon me to supply the want occasioned by what the general voice, less favourable than my own sentiments dispose me to feel towards him, does not scruple to call the deplorable inefficiency and incompetency of the Bishop.

"It is under these circumstances, and for these reasons, very reverend and illustrious sir, that I have felt it to be my duty to promote an inquiry into certain particulars of the character and conduct of the Superior, who was recently appointed to the government of the convent of Ursuline nuns in this city. And you will readily comprehend, very reverend and illustrious sir, that in taking all the circumstances of the case into my consideration, and being aware that the convent is honoured by having been selected by you as the temporary residence of your niece, the Signora Contessa Stella Altamari, I have felt it to be my duty to communicate to you the position of the community and the suspicions that attach to the character of the Superior. That person will in all probability very shortly be summoned by the ecclesiastical authorities to Florence, with a view to her deposition from the high office to which she was as unfortunately, as, I venture to think, inconsiderately, promoted; and as it has appeared to me probable that your illustrious reverence might think it desirable, under these circumstances, to recal your niece, I should therefore have shortly done myself the honour of writing to your reverence, even if the enclosed extraordinary letters had not fallen into my hands. Of course, when that occurred, I at once saw the propriety of forwarding them to you. As soon as the necessity of instituting an inquiry into the conduct of this strangely delinquent Superior became apparent, naturally one of the first steps to take was to intercept her correspondence. For a long time no light could be obtained by this means; for she received no letters. But at last my vigilance was rewarded by the possession of those herewith enclosed. I need not point out to your reverence the importance of them both as regards the possible antecedents of this dangerous woman, the truly abominable breach of trust of which she has been guilty with regard to your niece, and, lastly, as regards the conduct and views of the illustrious lady the Contessa Stella herself.

"Without presuming to enter into reflections on this latter part of the subject, I content myself with calling your reverence's prudent and experienced attention to the hopes and feelings expressed in the atrociously audacious letters of this man who signs himself Giulio Malatesta; and who, as far as I can gather from the letters themselves, and from such inquiries as I have been able to make, must be an illegitimate son of the Marchese Cesare Malatesta of Fermo. You will observe that this shameless vagabond proposes to present himself at the Ursuline convent here in Montepulciano. Should you think it expedient to obtain an order for his arrest, it might be easily executed on his putting his avowed intention into execution, without any difficulty or disturbance. All such considerations, however, together with any others, which the perusal of these infamous letters may suggest to the wisdom and prudence of your illustrious reverence, I leave to your high decision; and pass on without further encroaching on your valuable time, to the honour of subscribing myself,

"With sentiments of the most distinguished esteem and respect of your illustrious reverence, the most humble and devoted servant, and unworthy brother in Christ,

"DOMENICO TONDI,
"Cancel. Dioc. Montis Pul."

If the writers of the three letters which thus reached the hands of the Canonico Adalberto had been invisibly present when they were read by him, the Very Reverend the Chancellor of the Diocese of Montepulciano would have been the most dissatisfied with the result produced by the reading of them. Giulio's letters to his love and to the Abbess were read with great attention and considerable interest, which was marked by sundry pauses of meditation over their contents, and here and there a "humph," uttered more in the tone of a man considering his adversary's move in a game of chess, than of one excited to anger or even surprise.

"Well!" he muttered to himself, when he had come to the end of poor Giulio's letters, "let him find his mother, if he can. Upon the whole, it would be more likely to put another spoke in his wheel, and lend us a help, than the reverse! Likely enough that she may have been placed in a convent by the Cardinal. Not unlikely that this Abbess may have some knowledge of her! But what this old mad woman at Bologna—what is the name?—Varani—means by her sealed packet and her journey to France, who can guess? Any way, I don't think she is likely to help my young friend to marry the heiress of the Altamari! Her son, a Professor at Pisa! That is worth taking a note of. Possibly a little pressure on this gentleman, who is so excellent a friend of our young spark, may prove to be useful. Aha! so they count on our preferring to allow our heiress to marry a vagabond without a *sou* to seeing the property go to a distant heir! We shall find the means of dissipating *that* illusion very easily! And our young Bayard is going to make himself Generalissimo of the revolutionary army, and come to demand his bride when he is such a great man, that the Altamari will be only too proud of his alliance! Ha! ha! ha! And 'Italy has not said her last word yet!' *Per Dio!* No, my young friend! That has she not. And if you do not chance to be shot as a rebel taken in arms before your greatness comes upon you, why, then it will be time enough to think of giving up the game."

This was the train of thought produced in the brain of the scheming Canonico by the perusal of Giulio's letters; but when he finished reading the laboriously written epistle, the composition of which had cost his provincial brother Canon so much thought and pains, he tossed it aside with a "Pish!" and a muttered "Old fool! As if I had not known all he can tell me long ago! It would serve him right to send his letter to the Bishop! Only it would be a sin against the golden rule, 'Never do any man an ill turn, when there is nothing to be got by it!' It's just as well, though, that these letters have been intercepted before they reached their destination. And they show that the recal of this wilful little Contessina has been put off too long already. Our friend Bayard, the renegade King's Generalissimo *in posse*, thinks that her coming to Florence will give him an opportunity of seeing her here, as he is good enough to observe. We shall see!"

And, so musing, the Canonico Adalberto went off to the Palazzo Altamari to seek an interview with his sister-in-law. It was an earlier hour than that at which the Canon usually made his rare visits at the *palazzo*; for he had come immediately after reading his morning letters. He rarely came near the family *palazzo* at all, save on matters of business, as in the present instance, or on occasions of ceremonious visits, such as on New Year's-days, and birthdays, or name-days* rather, and such like. He was on this occasion shown into Zenobia's morning-room, where Mademoiselle Zélie shortly came to him, to tell him, with a very low curtsey, and standing just inside the door—for Zélie stood desperately in awe of the Canon, and considered him to be a sort of incarnation of the Inquisition—that the Signora Contessa would have much pleasure in seeing him in her chamber.

In fact, it was the sacred hour of the "*roovelly.*"

The Canon glanced at her, as he answered, "Is the Contessa ill, then, that she does not leave her chamber?"

He knew all about the "roovellies," as well as all about most other matters pertaining to his sister-in-law; but he had small tolerance for such absurdities; and but small liking for the French *soubrette* promoted to be a denizen of his ancestral *saloni.*

"Not ill, your reverence," said poor Zélie, colouring and curtseying again, and wishing herself anywhere but where she was—"not precisely ill! But her ladyship prefers to receive her morning visitors in a *toilette de chambre,*" continued

* People in Italy, as in other Catholic countries, make a holiday, not as we do of the anniversary of a birthday, but of the saint's day in the calendar who is the namesake of the individual.

Zélie, judiciously modifying the offensive words, "in bed," by that euphuism; and endeavouring still further to propitiate the terrible Canon by hastening to add, "such special visitors, at least, as her ladyship is desirous of treating with special distinction."

"Humph!" said the priest, with a grim smile; "has the Contessa any other old women or men with her now in her bedroom?"

"Your reverence!" said the little Frenchwoman, greatly shocked; "there are a few of her ladyship's habitués. The Marchese is there, of course; and there is the young Marchese Alfonso. I do not know if there are any others."

"Tell your——tell the Contessa," said the Canon, correcting himself, as he remembered Zélie's present rank in the household, "that I wish to speak with her on business; and that I will wait here till she ——rises above the horizon to the outer world," added the Canon, with a mocking smile; "I am not in the habit," he continued, as Zélie turned to the door right glad to escape, "of visiting ladies in their bedrooms;—at least," he added, with a smile to himself, when Zélie had already closed the door behind her, "not when there are others of the party."

The Canonico Adalberto did not wait many minutes before the Marchese Florimond came to him.

"*O stimatissimo** Signor Canonico!" exclaimed the little man, bustling into the room, and coming forward with both hands extended to meet the visitor; "the Contessa is shocked to keep your reverence waiting! You are early this morning! It is a *vero beneficio del cielo*† to see you so well! The Contessa was receiving a few friends in her chamber. It is her habit, you know. *Queste donne!*"‡—with a deprecatory shrug.

"Upon my word, Signor Marchese, I am glad it is no worse! When I heard that the Signora Contessa had her bedroom full of people, Heaven help me, I thought it must be the *santissimo*,§ and that the poor Contessa was *in extremis*. We priests, you know, naturally have our heads filled with the business of our trade!"

"God forbid!" exclaimed the Marchese, not a little shocked. "No! thanks to the Madonna, we are not come to that yet!"

"No, no! not yet!" answered the Canon, with a malicious emphasis on the words; "the Signora Contessa, as all Florence knows, is essentially an evergreen!"

* "Most esteemed." A common mode of address.

† "A true blessing of Heaven." A somewhat old-fashioned style of courtesy, which the present generation would deem provincial at least, if not under-bred.

‡ "These ladies!"

§ The last sacrament; at the administration of which, to dying persons, several individuals are generally present.

"Hah! Signor Canonico!" exclaimed the admirably got-up Marchese, with a shrug that seemed to lift him bodily up out of his boots, and bring his shoulders up to his ears, and his eyebrows up to his wig, "we all have sooner or later to grow old!"

"*Most* men have to do so!" replied the Canon, with a low bow to the Marchese. "*Most* men, Signor Marchese, *do* sooner or later grow old," he repeated, parodying the famous French preacher, who implied in similar fashion an exemption to the universality of human mortality in favour of Louis the Fourteenth!

But the Canon might have spared his irony for it was quite thrown away upon the dapper little Marchese, who only made a disclamatory grimace in reply, which seemed to express that what the Canon said was very true, but that his mode of mentioning it was too flattering.

"I wished to speak with the Contessa this morning about my niece, the Contessina Stella," the Canonico continued; "circumstances have arisen which appear to make the convent at Montepulciano no longer a desirable residence for her."

"Dear me! The Contessa will be much grieved to hear it," said the Marchese; "unless, indeed," he added, "we might hope that the Contessina Stella's residence in the convent has already produced the effect expected from it."

"I fear me," replied the Canon, "that there is as yet no ground for any such anticipation. The Contessina Stella has, it would seem, a strong will of her own, which can only be made to yield by the conviction that the wills opposed to it are yet stronger."

"And what would your reverence propose doing in the first instance?" asked the Marchese Florimond.

"My notion," said the priest, "would be to bring her home here at once; to profit by the opportunity to watch her narrowly, and ascertain whether her courage has been at all shaken; and, at the same time, never to allow her to lose sight of the fact, that submission is the only means of saving herself from a speedy return to life in a cloister."

"I am sure the Contessa will feel the wisdom of deferring to your opinion, Signor Canonico," replied the little man, anxious to avoid having to express any opinion before the Contessa should have given him his cue. "She will be here in a minute or two. If you will allow me, I will go and see whether she is coming."

And the Marchese escaped accordingly.

In a very few minutes he came back, accompanied by the Contessa Zenobia, who had evidently lost no time in dismissing her gentlemen of the bed-chamber, and preparing herself for the decorous reception of her formidable ecclesiastical brother-in-law.

She came into the room with a jerking, jaunty step, half dance, half hobble, exclaiming as soon as she was inside the door:

"*Ah! bone jouar, Monsieur le Canon! bone jouar! Vous êtes bien preste ce matin!*" said she, in her own peculiar language.

The Canon could speak French perfectly well, and was often not a little amused at his sister-in-law's *lingua franca*, as the Contessa's talk often deserved to be called in more senses than one. It was nothing new to him to be addressed by her as "*Monsieur le Canon*," though she sometimes varied her translation to "*Monsieur le Canonic;*" but he never gave her the pleasure of speaking French to her in return.

"Good morning, Signora!" he said; "my excuse for disturbing you so early must be found in the importance of the business on which I have to speak to you."

"*Ah! che cose! che cose!** The Marchese here has been telling me! To think of an Abbess having effected no good in all this time! She ought to cashiered, *per Bacco!*"

"But the more immediate question for us, Signora, seems to be, whether it would not be well to

* "What things! What things!"

bring the Contessina Stella home at once, before further mischief—or, indeed, I may say, before any serious mischief has been done?"

"What! bring her here to insult *ces braves garçons nos restaurateurs* again, and to turn up her nose at the Marchese Alfonso, *il poveraccio!** *Per Dio*, he will have enough of her when they are married, trust me, Monsieur le Canon, without frightening the poor creature out of his wits beforehand. I will tell you what it is, your reverence, we shall never bring him up to the scratch, let alone her, if we show them too much of each other!"

"Signor Contessa," said the churchman, "the profound prudence which dictates your observations is equalled only by the delicate tact with which they are expressed. But I did not intend to propose that the Contessina should be allowed to share in the brilliant society which you are celebrated for collecting around you. I would suggest, that, supposing, as we have reason to fear, that the young lady still shows herself obdurate, she should live for the short time which must intervene before we can find some proper asylum for her, entirely in her own chamber, and an adjoining room, on the second floor of the palace. This arrangement would give me also the opportunity to visit her oc-

* "The poor devil!"

casionally, and try whether the counsels and arguments I could lay before her might have the effect of bringing her to reason."

"I think you're right, Monsieur le Canon! I give my entire consent. There is nothing like preaching, to tire one's heart out! If you could stand it yourself—and you might get help for that matter—and would not mind giving her a dose of a couple of hours or so two or three times a day, depend upon it she would give in. I am sure I should consent to anything, if it was tried upon me!" added the fascinating, light-hearted little creature, with a shrill laugh.

"I am fully sensible of your too flattering appreciation of my humble powers, Signora! I shall not fail to do what I can. But we must not expect that all your sex are endowed to an equal extent with yourself with intellectual powers amenable to the force of reason."

"What will be the best plan, Signor Canonico, for bringing the Contessina home?" asked the Marchese Florimond, wishing to make a diversion, for he had a rather vague perception that the polished churchman was laughing at the fair Zenobia.

"I think I shall do well to go and bring her to Florence myself," replied the Canon, changing his tone to a simple business-like manner; "it may be," he added, "that I may pick up some information there that may be worth our having."

"And when would you propose making the journey?" rejoined the Marchese.

"With as little loss of time as possible. I am afraid we have been remiss in not taking the step earlier. I should hope to be here with the young lady by next Friday night."

So it was decided that Stella was to be brought back to Florence, preparatory to being sent off to some new place of confinement and moral torment, if she should still obstinately refuse to yield to the wishes of her family.

It made no part of the Canon Altamari's plan to enter in any way into the causes of complaint which he might have against the Abbess, and still less to meddle with the differences which might exist between her and her ecclesiastical superiors. The latter were supremely uninteresting to him; and as to the former, the Canon was one of those men who expend as little as possible of their energies on the past and irremediable. He was capable of any cruelty or oppression for the purpose of compelling another to submit to his will; but had no strong desire to inflict vengeance on any one for not having done so with regard to a matter which could not influence the future. Bygones were always absolutely bygones with him! He was an essentially practical man, and habitually turned all his thoughts and all his efforts to the future and the practicable, to the utter neglect of that which was already past, irrevocable, or out of his power.

The particular type of character described is a more common one in Italy than among ourselves, and may, perhaps, be especially often met with among the members of the priesthood.

It was also the purpose of the Canon Altamari to allow as little time as might be for any leave-taking between Stella and the Abbess. He hoped, moreover, by the suddenness of his operations at Montepulciano, to escape any interview with Don Domenico Tondi, which he instinctively felt would be supremely disagreeable to him.

There is nothing a Roman Catholic ecclesiastic, who is much of a gentleman, and very little of a priest, hates more than being brought into relations with a brother ecclesiastic who is very little a gentleman, and very much a priest.

It was a great and painful shock both to the Abbess and to Stella, when a letter from the Canon Altamari was brought one morning to the former, intimating that in about an hour he should have the honour of waiting on the Superior for the purpose of receiving his niece from her hands and conducting her to Florence. As it was uncertain, the letter stated, whether she would return to Montepulciano, the Canon requested that the hour which would elapse before he should have the pleasure of seeing her might be employed in making any preparation for her quitting the convent which might be necessary. It grieved him, the writer added, not to have been able to allow the convent and his niece a longer notice of her recal; but the necessary arrangements for the journey, and his own many and pressing avocations, must furnish his excuse.

It was a great shock, and the parting between the two women who had learned to love each other with all the clinging affection of two loving natures, enhanced by their common interest in the same individual, by the possession of a common secret, by mutual sympathy, and the sweet sharing of their sorrows and hopes and fears, by the ungenial environment which rendered them all in all to each other, was a very bitter one. For the Abbess it was worse even than for Stella. The latter, though she had no reason to hope that the intentions of her family were in any degree changed with regard to her, or to expect any mitigation of the means that would be adopted to compel her submission to those intentions, was at least about to emerge from her cloister-grave into the living world, and the change suggested a whole chapter of possibilities. The former, with the newly-awakened and painfully-vibrating consciousness of affections and interests, which had been dead for so many years, was to be left to the utter solitude of heart, which her recent companionship with Stella had taught her once again to feel as a horrible and fearful desolation. The pang which she had endured when her heart was first rent asunder from all its human ties, had to be undergone anew, and the lethargic torpidity of the twenty intervening years to be reached again, athwart a new apprenticeship of suffering.

There was to be added to all this the minor but not inconsiderable source of sorrow and trouble arising from the sense of isolation, and the consciousness that she was an object of dislike and suspicion to the sisterhood. She was not aware of the extent to which this hostility had already proceeded, and could still less imagine that she was the object of an organised system of *espionnage*, which had been pushed to the extent of intercepting her correspondence. But it was impossible to avoid being aware that no confidence or friendly feeling existed between herself and the members of the community she was called on to govern.

The parting, too, between the Abbess and Stella was unalleviated by any of those mitigations which make most partings, save that resulting from death, more tolerable. It was difficult to look forward to any future meeting, and not less so to indulge in the hope of any correspondence by letter. With so much between them, respecting which each of them would long so to hear tidings from the other, with so many common hopes and fears trembling in the balance, the inexorable convent gate which was to shut in the one and shut out the other, would be even as the stone at the mouth of the sepulchre between them!

But there was no possibility of struggling against the will and fiat of the Canon, which was as the doom of fate to these two helpless women.

On Friday, the 5th of March, as he had said, the Canon arrived in Florence with his niece, and brought her safely to the palace in the Via Larga, where she was at once consigned, under the pitying but incorruptible gaolership of Zélie, to her prison, consisting of the two rooms on the second floor, as her uncle had suggested.

Some little time elapsed before the Canonico Adalberto was able to find a convent in all respects suitable to his views, to which Stella might be again consigned. It will be easily understood that many points had to be considered in making the selection—the nature of the rule, the character of the Superior, to a certain degree even that of the sisterhood, the locality, the jurisdiction, &c. At length, however, the difficulties arising from all these requirements were surmounted, and it was announced to Stella, that if she still continued obdurate, she would be sent, with a view of shortly commencing her novitiate, to a convent in the little town of Palazzuolo. The position exactly answered to all the Canon wished, and was selected with the judicious skill of one fully aware of the powerful influence exercised by the imagination over the mind, especially of a young girl left in total solitude of the mind and heart. It is hardly possible to conceive a more desolate position than that occupied by the little frontier town in question. Situated on the eastern slope of the main chain of the Apennine, near the northern frontier of Tuscany, where it confines with the Papal territory, it is lost amid the arid and storm-swept flanks of the mountains, distant alike from any of the larger centres of population, and from any of the great lines of communication. Nobody ever "passes through" Palazzuolo. None come there, save those very few to whom it is the end and object of their journey. All the circumstances of the place and its surroundings are well calculated to work on the imagination of an exile among these dreary hills, and impress the victim with the hopelessness of her position.

But it was, as has been said, some time before this favourable spot was discovered by the Canon, and eventually it was decided that Stella was to be consigned to her new prison on the 1st of June. Her uncle did not regret the delay. For, although he did not purpose trying his preaching powers on his niece exactly after the fashion suggested by the Contessa Zenobia, he *did* think it well to ascertain the state of her mind, and see how far it might be possible for his own to influence it. It formed no part of the polished Canon's purpose to descend to violent threats or reproaches in his interviews with his niece, and still less to endeavour to move her by hypocritically unctuous appeals to the sanctions of duty and religion. His plan was simply to allow the hopelessness of resistance to sink into her mind, to convince her by words dropped here and there with apparent carelessness, and by taking the matter for granted, rather than by violent declarations, that there was not the smallest possibility that any other alternative was before her save obedience or the veil.

We may be very sure that even if he had succeeded in convincing Stella of this, he would have failed in his object. She would have chosen the latter rather than the former alternative. Marriage with the Marchese Alfonso! Would not death itself be preferable! But Stella had a great comfort and support in the declaration of the Abbess, that she could not be made a nun without her own acceptance of that fate. She had little doubt, however, that she might be doomed to an indefinitely prolonged imprisonment; and, on the whole, it must be admitted that the period of nearly three months which Stella had to pass in durance and disgrace, varied only by the visits of her Aunt Zenobia and her uncle, the Canon—of which it is but justice to the Canon to say that those by the lady were by far the more intolerable infliction—was a trial of her constancy and courage by no means less arduous than her convent experiences.

CHAPTER V.

GIULIO IN FLORENCE ONCE MORE.

While the dull, slow months were dragging wearily on with Stella in her prison in the Palazzo of the Via Larga, and bringing her nearer and nearer to the fated first of June, which was to be the limit of her stay in Florence, they had been passing more rapidly and busily with Giulio.

Not so the first of them, however. For, during nearly the whole of March he had been obliged to await idly in Bologna the daily-expected death of old Marta Varani. She lingered on from day to day, in contradiction to all the previsions of the medical man, for almost a month from the time of the interview that has been described between her and Giulio. He saw her twice in the course of that time, and would have done so oftener, had not the strange and unkindly-natured old woman given him very clearly to understand that she preferred being left alone. She was not entirely so, however; for Giulio by chance discovered that she was occasionally visited by one or two of her old political friends. He had asked her at one of these interviews if it would be a comfort to her to have her son summoned from Pisa. But she had said that it was useless;—that she should be gone before the letter could reach Pisa;—that she and Pietro had never had much to say to each other, and would have less than ever now!

"Tell him, when you see him," she said, "what I bade you;—that my last act was to sacrifice a life-long object because I thought that he would wish me to do so. That is all that need pass between him and me!"

Giulio, however, had written from Bologna to the Professor, telling him the condition in which his mother was, and the improbability that he could find her alive, if, despite of what she had said, he should attempt to come to her. He told him also the strangely mysterious message with which he was charged, and all the history of the still more mysterious packet. And he had received letters from the Professor in return, in which he had declared his inability to throw the smallest light upon any part of the matter. He knew that his mother had once lived in the south of France, and could only guess that she might have kept up some correspondence with persons there for political purposes. But what bearing this could by any possibility have on any part of his friend Malatesta's affairs or interests, he was utterly at a loss to imagine.

At length the old woman died. And the next two months of the three which Stella had to pass in listening to the passionate scolding of her Aunt Zenobia, varied only by the visits, and smooth, polished, iron-like impassibility of her uncle, were much more active ones for Giulio.

The contents of the packet, the seal of which, as may be easily imagined, he lost no time in breaking as soon as he was privileged to do so, did not in any wise tempt him to delay the journey into the south of France which he had been enjoined to make. On the contrary, the statement of facts which he found therein made him doubly anxious to be on his road. And when the journey had been prosperously performed, and the information obtained which he was sent to seek, anxious as he was to make his promised visit to Montepulciano, he found himself obliged by the circumstances that had become known to him to return immediately to Bologna, and give his attention to certain business there, which occupied him for several days.

At last, after all these delays, he was able, towards the end of May, to hasten to Montepulciano;—only to learn on his arrival there that the Superior of the convent of Ursulines had been some weeks previously summoned to Florence.

Having very little doubt, from the last letters he had had from Carlo Brancacci, that Stella had also ere this been recalled home, he thought it more prudent to risk no inquiry about her, but once again set out with as little delay as possible for Florence. There his first object was to see Carlo Brancacci, which he hoped to do on the morning of his arrival. For, having pushed on from Montepulciano in time to reach Siena before the diligence from Rome passed through, about nightfall, on its northern journey, his plan was, by travelling all night, as the diligence in those days did between Siena and Florence, to reach the latter city early in the morning.

The diligence was due in Florence at five o'clock A.M.; and as it had been a lovely moonlight night, and the excellent road was in the best possible condition, and the journey had been in all respects a prosperous one, the vehicle managed to reach the Porta Romana by six, and was deemed by all parties concerned, including the boastful conductor, to have achieved an admirable amount of punctuality.

Com' è gentil
*La notte a mezzo April!**

says the Italian libretto. And though, as the seasons now are in Tuscany, it might require a considerable dose of romance to make any one, save an expectant lover, find it charming to lounge at midnight *sub Dio* exactly at that season, it was some six weeks later in the year at the time of Giulio's journey, and the nights might then, indeed, be said to be delightful! He had shared the "*banquette*" on the top of the carriage with the conductor, and had, in truth, enjoyed his daybreak descent from the Chianti hills too much to regret the extra hour, even if it ever entered into the head of an Italian to dream of being discontented at such a circumstance!

Giulio had much in his mind which disposed him not to be discontented with any of the things or circumstances around him. The precise nature of the facts of which he had recently become aware will be more conveniently, for the purposes of narration, communicated to the reader in a future chapter; but it may be stated, in the mean time, that they were of such a kind as, despite the hitherto unsuccessful search after his mother, and despite the difficulties which interposed themselves between him and Stella, sent him to Florence in a

* How charming is the night in the middle of April.

happier and more hopeful state of mind than had ever yet been his since that memorable first day of Lent on which he had last quitted it, now three years ago. There lay before him much in that beautiful city towards which he was descending that was fraught with anxiety; but it was a hopeful anxiety, which partook more of the nature of eagerness than of fear.

The view of the city from the hills, crossed by the old Roman road, is a charming one, as, indeed, every approach to the City of Flowers from the surrounding hills must be. But it is not one of the most beautiful, or at least not one of the most perfect views of the Val d'Arno, and the fair city in the midst of it. In vain, as the principal of the monumental edifices of the city opened on his view, did Giulio endeavour to make out the long line of the Via Larga, and to fancy the spot in it where the Palazzo Altamari contained the treasure that made life bright and valuable to him. Somewhere—in some sacred spot beneath that labyrinth of grey-red roofs, now being lit up and gilded into picturesque beauty by the rising sun—was sleeping, he trusted, calmly and securely, if not quite happily sleeping, his beloved one! Dreaming—of what? That her latest waking thoughts and her prayers had been of him and for him, he was well assured. Did any mysterious influence of affinity warn her in her dreams of his approach near and nearer to her? Were, even now, those morning dreams, that come true, it is said, warning her of his coming, and of the possibilities which the tidings he was bringing with him would open before them?

The diligence, as has been said, was deemed by all parties concerned to have done wonders in that it had arrived at the Porta Romana at six A.M., only one hour after the time it ought to have reached the end of its journey. But to have reached the city gate was a very different thing from this, as all continental travellers by diligence, in what may already happily be called the olden times, know by sufficiently disagreeable reminiscences.

Having succeeded in bringing the huge machine up to the gateway in a sharp trot, commenced two or three hundred yards off, with an amount of exertion, and bustle, and noise, which seemed to indicate that every instant was of the last importance, and pulled up their horses beneath the sombre old arch, under which so long a procession of monarchs, popes, cardinals, warriors, armies, statesmen, ambassadors, spies, prisoners, and other notabilities have passed during the last five hundred years, the postilions dismounted from their horses, and proceeded to light their cigars preparatory to a lounging chat with the loiterers about the gate, in a manner which indicated plainly enough that the care and business of life were off their minds for some time to come. The conductor, on the contrary, roused himself to a state of intense activity and bustle. For the terrible ordeal of the octroi was to be passed. All articles of consumption, meat, bread, butter, wine, oil, &c., are taxed on entering within the city wall. And who could say that some infinitesimal quantity of some one of these articles,—even an entire bottle of wine possibly,—might not lurk in the profundities of some traveller's trunk, and the Grand-Ducal revenues be thus defrauded of some fraction of a penny! Therefore the entire laboriously built-up arrangement of the mountain of baggage and goods on the roof has to be laboriously undone, and the entire component parts, therefore, scattered about the pavement. It is true, that any such examination of the heterogeneous assemblage of packages as would really serve to ascertain that no specimen of the articles sought for was hidden within them, would probably occupy the entire day;—that no such examination was attempted; —that the officials contented themselves in most instances with opening the various trunks and closing them again, so that no object of any sort was attained by the process, save a certain amount of injury to the articles, a certain amount of torment to their proprietors, and the delay of an hour added to the long and tedious journey. Still there were advantages in the institution that were not to be despised by a sage and paternal government. In the first place, a considerable number of officials had to be maintained at each gate of the city for the management of the operation; and thus the number of persons interested in the maintenance of the government was increased; and, in the second place, all travelling was discountenanced and rendered difficult and disagreeable; —a consideration never lost sight of by rulers, who deem, not unreasonably, that the more nearly their people can be induced to remain in the condition of *adscripti glebæ*, the safer and better established is their rule.

Giulio had with him but a valise, which he could with the greatest ease have taken in his hand, and made the best of his way at once to his inn, leaving his more impeded fellow-travellers to endure the delay with what patience they might. But he was an Italian, and far too well broken in to Italian ways and rules to think of attempting anything of the sort. No such escape from the troubles of the gate would have been permitted. Having cast in his lot with the diligence, it was imperative to partake its fortunes even to the end. And that end was not attained at the office close to the Piazza Santa Trinità, in the centre of the town, till half-past seven. And it took Giulio about another hour before he had found quarters in one of the old-fashioned inns behind the Palazzo Vecchio; and having changed his dress, and got a cup of coffee at a neighbouring café, set forth in search of his friend Brancacci.

It was about half-past eight, therefore, when he passed through the Piazza della Signoria—or the Piazza del Gran-Duca, as it was called in those days—on his way towards the Via Larga. He thought, as he crossed that centre and heart of Florence, that there was a certain air of something more than usual being about to happen in the city. There seemed to be more people astir than was usually the case, save on a holiday. And the day of his arrival, the 29th of May, was not any holiday, that he was aware of. There was that indescribable appearance of somewhat out of the train of their every-day thoughts and occupations being in the minds of the people, which always may be observed in any town where some unusual event or solemnity is in hand. And Giulio was looking round him, as he was passing out at that corner of the great square at which the Via dei Calzainoli opens, in search of some one of whom he might ask the meaning of this unwonted movement, when whom should he see coming towards him across the front of the Post-office from the Via Vacchereccia, at the other corner of the Piazza, but Rinaldo Palmieri.

They both caught sight of each other at the same moment, and, running forward, met beneath that beetling brow of the old *Tetto dei Pisani*,—that roof which the Florentines of old compelled their Pisan captives to build, and which now shelters their descendants while they are asking for their letters at the post-office.

"What, Giulio in Florence!"

"Rinaldo! What luck to meet you!"

"How long have you been here?"

"Just arrived, of course! Not an hour ago! Would you not have seen me otherwise, my dear fellow!"

"And where have you been? What have you been doing? Where do you come from? What brings you to Florence? But of course you have come for to-day. And you have done well!"

"What do you mean? But, first, how is your wife? And what news of the Professor?"

"All well! thanks! The Professor is in Florence. You did not think the dear old fellow would miss the day, did you?"

"Miss what day? I saw there was something in the wind; but I have no idea what it is all about!"

"What!" cried Rinaldo, looking at him with the most unfeigned astonishment, "you don't mean it! You don't mean to say that you don't know—— Pooh! I can't believe it!"

"Believe what? I have not the least notion of what you are talking about! Remember that I am only half an hour old in Florence."

"But I took it for granted that you had come on purpose! Why, man alive! is it not the 29th of May? Have *you*, of all the people in the world, forgotten all about Curtatone?"

"No, *davvero!*"* But I had not thought of this day being the anniversary of it!"

"And you reach Florence this morning by mere chance! *O bella!*"†

"And all this stir in the streets is about that!"

"*Altro!*‡ I should think there was a stir too! But whither were you bound when we met?"

"To the Via Larga, to find Brancacci. I hope he is in Florence!"

"Yes! He is here. But you can't go to the Via Larga now! There is other work cut out for you this morning!"

"What, the anniversary? What is to take place?"

"Ay! that is the question! What is to take place?" returned Rinaldo, changing his tone to one of concentrated earnestness. "That is what

* "In truth."

† A common exclamation, nearly equivalent to "Only to think of that!"

‡ "Ay! and more than that!"

we shall see, Giulio *mio!* You must come with me now to Santa Croce. Finding Brancacci, or any other business, let it be what it may, must come after that. Come along! I will tell you how things are as we go. We shall find Francesca and the Professor there."

So, hooking his arm within that of Giulio, he led him off in the direction of the church of Santa Croce, towards which, as they neared that part of the city, it became evident that the tide of people was strongly setting. For more than one feeling was leading the Florentines on this, the third anniversary of the battles of Curtatone and Montanara, to the church, in which the names of those who fell on that day had been commemorated.

The hopes of Italy had sadly fallen since that time. The Carnival was over. The high and serene masquers had pulled off their Phrygian caps, and other such disguisements; and having thus changed their mood, insisted that their peoples should follow their lead, forget their mumming, and fall back into the old ruts and tramways. An Austrian garrison was in occupation of Florence, at the invitation of that Grand-Duke who had sent out the Tuscan volunteers to fight against the Austrians in Lombardy three short years ago! Only three short years! But the Grand-Duke had in that time seen the error of his ways during that short period of carnival madness. His repentance was sincere; and Austria had forgiven him. But he did not like to be reminded of the follies of which he had repented. Nobody does like it. If the Tuscan lads, who had left their lives on the battle-fields of Lombardy, had taken the liberalising mood of their paternal sovereign so much in earnest, so much the worse for them. In any case, all that chapter of incidents had better be forgotten now. It is in ill taste, unfashionable, and very displeasing to paternal rulers to say or do anything that can recal the memory of all that already buried and forgotten past. With our Austrian friends here in Florence too! Nothing could be so "*inconvenable!*"

But the fathers, mothers, brothers, sisters, and beloved ones of the youths, who had left their young lives on those not-to-be-mentioned battle-fields, did not feel quite in unison with the courtly tone of sentiment on this subject. Immediately after that sad but glorious campaign, before Curtatone and Montanara were tabooed names in Florence, a couple of bronze tablets, recording the names and ages of the slain in those two battles, had been put up in Santa Croce;—the Tuscan Westminster Abbey. And on the anniversary of the battle, the families and friends of these lost ones had caused a requiem to be celebrated in memory of them, and of their deeds, and had brought chaplets and flowers to lay before the bronze record, as a testimony that the memory of the dead was yet green in the hearts of those who had loved them.

In 1849, this commemoration of what it would fain forget, was distasteful to the paternal government. In 1850, it was yet more offensive. And now, in 1851, these uncourtly mourners, with their inopportune reminiscences, were purposing to repeat the offence! Totally regardless of the feelings of their Grand-Duke, surrounded by a circle of Austrian marshals and generals, yet at the same time compelled to endure under his nose the commemoration of those whom he had sent out to fight against those marshals and generals, they persisted in refusing to forget! Incapable as they were of any courtly delicacy of feeling, these burgher mourners even went to the length of sending an invitation to the Austrian commander-in-chief to be present at their celebration. And he, being more soldier than courtier, as it would seem, wrote back to say that, though prevented by political considerations from attending the ceremony in question, he should be with them in heart, and was glad to have the opportunity of expressing the high respect and admiration which every soldier must feel for the gallant youths who had shown themselves such worthy foemen.

If only the Austrian commander could have

had the tact to use his supreme authority to forbid any such commemoration! But since he took it in the tone he did, the paternal government could scarcely do so! It was supremely unpleasant to a paternal ruler!

And thus it came to pass, that now on that beautiful May morning, the question was, as Rinaldo had said to Giulio, "what would take place?" Would the government venture on shutting up the church? Would it content itself with ordering the priests to celebrate no service? Would it abstain from any interference, and bear its mortification in silence, as best it might?

So Florence was astir, and uneasy with expectation and doubt. The patriots of 1848, those who had lost relatives on that day in the first line, were thronging towards the church; the few partisans of the court were biting their nails in sulky and uneasy groups at street corners, the merely curious crowd of quidnuncs was hovering about the squares in timid doubt, and the Austrian officers were clanking their swords up and down the pavement, very indifferent to all that the children they were sent to keep in order were making such a fuss about, but ready to compel them to be orderly by a very rough and ready process, in case their quarrelling should go to the extent of a breach of the peace.

All this state of things Rinaldo explained rapidly to Giulio as they were walking from the Piazza della Signoria to the Piazza di Santa Croce; to the exceeding indignation of the latter. His impression, however, was that the government would take no steps to prevent the commemoration.

"They cannot do it, *caro mio!* It is impossible. That move of inviting the Austrian commandant was admirably thought of. He must be a fellow with a soldier's heart in him.* And the style of his answer must make it impossible for them to interfere."

"I trust it may be so! We shall soon see! But I have not asked you anything about yourself yet."

"And I have so much to tell, that there is no time for it now! It must keep till after the ceremony. You shall then come with me to look for Brancacci. I have some things to tell you that will make you stare. I am in Fortune's good books at last, for a wonder, it would seem!"

* The general in question was Prince Frederick of Lichtenstein. The letter he sent in return to the invitation is so creditable to all parties concerned, save the Grand-Ducal government, and it places the conduct of the latter in so just and strong a light, that I have thought it well to give it entire at the end of the chapter. For the sake of historical accuracy, it may be mentioned, though the fact makes no difference to any appreciation of the circumstances, that the letter was written on occasion of the commemoration of 1850; whereas the scene related in the text occurred, as there represented, in 1851.

"*Per Bacco!* I have considered you so for some time past, Signor Giulio, on more counts than one! You can't have it all your own way, and all at once, you know! But I want to hear your new good news. Can't you out with it at once?"

"No, by no means! there is far too much of it! And I want to attend to the business in hand now. By Jove! what a crowd!" he exclaimed, as at that moment they came out from one of the narrow streets into the Piazza of Santa Croce. "The Florentines are doing us Curtatone boys the honour of making a great affair of our anniversary. Why, half the town is on foot!"

In fact, the whole of the large *piazza* before the western front of the venerable church seemed to be full of people. A Florentine crowd is always quiet and orderly; but on the present occasion they appeared to be even more so than usual; for a certain air of hushed quietude and almost of depression seemed to weigh upon the multitude, which indicated very sensibly that the great majority of those present were under the influence of the spirit of the occasion which called them together. Very many were in mourning garments. A stil greater number bore about them some token of mourning in some part of their dress. There was an unusually large proportion of women among those assembled; and here and there among the crowd might be observed individuals, mostly women, with chaplets of evergreens or of flowers in their hands. The grand old church—grand rather from the noble associations and reminiscences connected with it, than from any real architectural grandeur, save that of vast size—did not then possess the handsome marble façade which now, with perhaps somewhat too garish a smartness, decks the time-honoured building. The rough, unfinished brick front, which had been tolerated by so many generations of Florentines, that, despite its ugliness, they had almost come to love its hoary and homely boldness better than any completion, however perfect, of the original design, still looked down upon the large open space, and on the quaint and varied architecture of the old houses, which form its three other sides, as it used to do in the old days when in times of civic revel wild beasts were "hunted," as the old chroniclers have it, or baited rather, as we should call it, on this *piazza*.

The whole of one end of the oblong space is occupied by this wide front of the great church—wider than even that of the *duomo*. And the three huge doors in it, which were all open, and through all of which the multitude was streaming into the enormous interior of the church, seemed to swallow up the thousands into the cavernous gloom within, while no appreciable progress was being made towards filling it.

"The church is open, at all events!" said Giulio, as the two young men made their way up the middle of the *piazza*, towards the great door. "I think you will find that the government have no intention of meddling with you."

"I really begin to hope so too," returned Rinaldo. "I see no signs of either soldiers or police. And, in truth, when one comes to consider the thing in its entirety, it does seem almost too outrageous that any government on earth should seek to prevent the relatives and friends of those who have fallen in its service from commemorating them!"

"It does so, indeed. Where are you to find the Professor?"

"He, and my wife with him, were to be at the entrance of the cloister on the right-hand side of the church front. They will be there by this time."

And, in fact, in front of the cloister door, the two friends, when they had pushed a little farther through the crowd in that direction, descried the Professor and his sister waiting, and anxiously watching the aspect of the rapidly-thickening crowd. Francesca had a large and elaborate garland, of bay mingled with white roses, hanging on her arm, an intended tribute to the memory of Enrico, whose name on the bronze tablets indicated him as having been the youngest of the youthful band of martyrs at Curtatone and Montanara.

Had Giulio seen Francesca alone, as she stood there with the wreath in her hand, he would probably have failed to recognise her, so wholly different was the figure of the Florentine *sposa* from that of the volunteer from whom he had parted at Curtatone. It is true that he had known her first, and for a longer time, in the proper habiliments of her sex at Pisa. But the few short months of the Lombard campaign had been filled with events of a kind that leave so deep a mark in the memory, and the impressions of that memorable time so effectually obliterated those of the days before it, that for Giulio the idea of the Professor's sister was that of the handsome volunteer soldier, rather than of the pretty girl of the lone house in the fields of Pisa. Francesca, moreover, was no longer the same in appearance as she had been then. Marriage makes a notable and subtle difference in the *manière d'être* of a woman in every part of the world, but nowhere more so than in Italy, where the change from the chrysalis state of girlhood to the full-fledged dignity of matronhood—the right to the complimentarily-used title of *sposa*—is a very marked one.

Francesca, however, would have instantly recognised Malatesta, even if he had not been with her husband. Not that the three years which had passed since they had seen each other had made no difference in him. Far from it. The bearing of the captain of Lancers in the service of his Majesty the King of Sardinia was sufficiently different from that of the volunteer student. But in costume Giulio looked much the same as she had known him in old days at Pisa. For it must not be imagined that he was travelling either in the Papal dominions or in those of the Grand-Duke of Tuscany in the uniform of the Piedmontese service. That, in the change which had come over the dream of Italy since 1848, would have been quite out of the question.

So Francesca, sharply nudging the Professor's elbow to call home his wits, which were roaming among the throng as it was streaming past them into the church, stepped forwards to meet Rinaldo and his companion as they came up.

"Yes! you may well jump!" said her husband. "There was nothing else at the post! But there I found this gentleman, for all the world as if he had arrived, addressed, 'To be left till called for; this side uppermost!' Think of his having come to Florence this morning—this morning, of all the mornings in the year;—and he of all men in the world—in total oblivion and unconsciousness of what day it is, and asking innocently what all the movement in the streets is about! *Pare impossibile!**"

"The case is not quite so bad as he makes it out,

* "It seems impossible!" a very common expression of surprise.

Signora Francesca," said Giulio, laughing, and cordially shaking hands first with her and then with the Professor; "I have not forgotten Curtatone, friends, nor has Italy! *Per Dio, Nò!* and so these gentry will find out one of these days," nodding, as he spoke, at a couple of white-coated Austrian soldiers who strolled lazily past them, gazing wonderingly and amusedly at the crowd. "No! my forgetfulness was limited to the fact that to-day was the—for us, dear friends—ever sacred 29th of May. You see, I have been scouring the country in all directions on business of my own, and I have a pretty big budget full to tell you all as soon as we have a quiet hour, and I came here selfishly thinking of no affairs but my own; and, with better good fortune than I deserve, come in for to-day's celebration."

"No! I do not think that you will be one of the first to forget Curtatone, Signor Capitano!" said Francesca, glancing up with a quiver on her lip and a meaning look into Malatesta's face. "For one day," she added, with a sad smile, "you must be Signor Caporale once again! Ah! how all the incidents of that day come back to me in talking to you, Signor Giulio!" she continued, pressing her hands over her eyes as she spoke.

Malatesta answered her only by putting out his hand, and a second time exchanging a friendly grasp.

"I was thankful to you, Signor Giulio, for your

letters from Bologna," said the Professor; "it was a comfort to me to know that you were there. *Povera madre!* She, too, did her part for our Italy!"

"We shall have much to talk over together, dear old friend!" answered Giulio. "I owe you and La Signora Varani, *buon anima sua*,* more than you think for!"

"You will return with us after the ceremony in the church, will you not, Signor Capitano?" said Francesca, "we have all so much to say to each other! You know, of course, that La Contessina is in Florence?" she added, in an under tone, with a quick look up into his face.

He answered her by a silent nod, while Rinaldo said:

"Of course you will return with us, Signor Giulio. My mother will be so glad to see you. She has not forgotten, poor soul, that she owed it to you that she had one son's life to give for Italy."

"Of course I should have hurried to the house I remember so well, even if I had not fallen in with you all so fortunately. I looked up at it as I passed in the diligence this morning; and I will come in in the course of the afternoon. But my first business after the ceremony must be to find out Brancacci, as I was on my way to do when I met Rinaldo."

* Literally, "her good soul;" a common mode of parlance in mentioning persons who have died.

"You have not told us yet even, whence you now come," said Rinaldo. "You passed before my mother's window coming in through the Porta Romana? Then you are not now from Bologna?"

"No! I came last from Montepulciano. But, as I said, I must keep my story till after the ceremony, for it is a long one," replied Malatesta.

"At least tell us in one word whether you have succeeded in your search?" asked the Professor. "We know that your journey to Montepulciano must have been a fruitless one."

"Yes; alas! my trip to Montepulciano has availed me nothing. And I have not been successful in my search as yet. But I have found what I was not looking for, and little dreamed of finding," replied Malatesta, looking round from one to the other of his three friends. "But positively," he added, laughing, "you shall not tempt me to open my budget of news till I have time to empty it comfortably! Is it not time for us to go into the church? The crowd are all pouring in!"

"Yes! come! let us go in!" said Rinaldo. "It must be nearly the hour for the beginning of the service. And, *per Bacco!* the old church must be nearly full by this time!"

Nevertheless, it was not the case that *all* the crowd had entered the church, though a continuous stream had been passing in while the above conversation had been going on. For as the four friends went up the steps of the church, to reach the door of the southern side-aisle, they looked back on the large *piazza*, and saw that it still seemed nearly full of people. Most of these, however, were no doubt only idlers, drawn thither by curiosity to see whether the government would, as had been thought likely, interfere in any way to stop the celebration of the anniversary. Those more really interested in it, were no doubt pretty well all by this time in the church. And when the little party, who had not before been together since the day they had separated on the field of Curtatone, passed into the vast building, it seemed closely filled.

PRINCE LICHTENSTEIN'S LETTER TO GENERAL DE LAUGIER.

"I should have been extremely sorry if, out of consideration for us, you had neglected to celebrate the religious ceremony commemorative of those who fought and died bravely. The Tuscan troops did their duty in fighting. They obeyed the orders of their sovereign. The sole reproach we can make to them is, that they fought far better than we should have wished. If I do not take the liberty of assisting at the mass, it is in order to avoid, as much as I can, the chance of exciting the susceptibilities of such as have the name of honour on their lips but not in their heart. For, having had occasion to admire the bravery of our adversaries on the 29th of May, I should have esteemed myself honoured, as a soldier, by assisting at it. I abstain from it solely in order not to give an opportunity to fools to make it a cause of accusation against you, by attributing to it a cause very different from the true soldierly feeling which would induce me to do so. Pray accept on the vigil of the anniversary of the day on which I had the honour first to know you, the assurance of the high esteem in which I hold you.

"LICHTENSTEIN."

CHAPTER VI.

THE REQUIEM IN SANTA CROCE.

The Florentine people for many generations have held the church of Santa Croce in especial affection;—*affection* rather than *veneration*, which would be the word in most cases more appropriate to describe that special feeling attached to certain localities, which the Roman Catholic religion so much encourages. In every Roman Catholic city,—and almost in every village,—there are churches, or chapels, or oratories, or altars, to which a special and exceptional degree of holiness and sanctity are supposed to appertain, and which are therefore regarded with a special and exceptional degree of reverence. But this has no connexion with the sentiment with which the Florentine citizen regards Santa Croce. Florence is not, and never was, a very religious city. Even in the "ages of faith," and of ecclesiastical ascendancy, that "most republican of republics" was always ready to subordinate ecclesiastical and religious considerations to those of civil expediency and patriotism, in a manner that was generally unknown in those centuries. The church of Santa Croce, on the other hand, makes no especial claim to any exceptional sanctity. Of course it has the usual decent supply of sacred relics in sufficient quantity for the due performance of religious observances. But it possesses none of those extra holy articles or reminiscences, which constitute the reputation and the wealth of so many other fanes of far less celebrity.

The sentiment with which the Florentine regards Santa Croce, is a civil rather than a religious sentiment. And the presence beneath its enormous roof, which is most influentially active in his heart and mind, is less that which is symbolised by the host in its ostensory on the altar, than that of the mighty memories of those whose dust reposes beneath the flagstones. It is, as it has often been called, the Westminster Abbey of Florence. And the feeling with which an ordinary Florentine citizen enters it, is stronger than that experienced by an ordinary Englishman on entering Westminster Abbey, in proportion to the comparative smallness of the community affected by it, and the consequently greater personal share which every man has in the common possession.

There is little or nothing of the material beauty, which Westminster Abbey possesses in so eminent a degree, at Santa Croce. No other sentiment competes in the mind of him, who passes from the external southern sunshine into the cavern-like gloom of its huge nave, with that of reverence for the mighty dead around. There are a few rich painted windows in the chancel and transepts, there are a few—a very few—fragments of mediæval art; but, on the whole, the church of Santa Croce is very singularly poor in aught of beautiful or of artistic interest. The monumental sculpture is almost all below criticism. The cenotaph, which vainly strives, by accumulation of tons of marble, to obliterate the memory of the fact that Dante's dust does not sleep below, would be a disgrace to Kensal Green, and if transferred to St. Paul's would elevate by contrast the sculpture there to high art! The naked rafters of the wholly unornamented roof give a barn-like appearance to the entire edifice. There is, in truth, no element of beauty or grandeur, save vast size. Yet even the stranger from the northern side of the Alps walks the inscribed flagstones of Santa Croce with bated breath, and a consciousness of awed reverence, which he has rarely before experienced. The spell of mighty names is on him; and the air he is breathing seems laden with the most precious and imperishable memories of the past.

If such be the impression made upon a stranger, it will be readily understood that it is difficult to exaggerate the feeling with which the Florentine regards Santa Croce.

Almost the whole of the great length of the church is occupied by the enormous nave and side-aisles. The transept is large; but it crosses the nave quite at the eastern end of it, leaving the choir and chancel disproportionately small and insignificant. It is as if the preponderance of the civil element, which has been described as prevailing in the sentiment inspired by the church, entered also into the material construction of it. The division of the building specially belonging to and affected to the uses of the clergy is very small, and that apportioned to the people disproportionately large. On either side of the chancel are other chapels opening off the transept almost as large as the chancel itself. At the extremity of the southern transept there is a chapel on a raised floor, reached by flights of steps, the space beneath which is occupied by a lumber-room or workshop approached from the exterior of the church. At the extremity of the northern transept is a communication with the sacristy and with the cloisters, and the conventual buildings attached to the church. There is also a large chapel on the western side of either transept opening off it; and at the point where the nave joins the transept, the pavement is raised to the extent of one or two shallow steps, so that the whole floor of the latter part of the church is a little higher than that of the former.

The bronze tablets recording the names and ages of those who fell at Curtatone and Montanara, which have been already mentioned, are affixed to the eastern wall of the southern transept, between the entrance to the chancel, and the opening of one of the chapels on the south side of it.

The immense nave and side-aisles of the church were very full, when the little party, whose conversation has been recorded in the last chapter, entered it. A Tuscan crowd, however closely packed, is always not only orderly, but singularly good tempered and courteous. It is sufficient for any one to manifest a desire to pass through it, for every facility to be offered by the immediate bystanders to the operation. The prominent feeling in the mind of an Englishman in such a position is, that he has as good a right as another to occupy his standing ground, and that he will not, therefore, permit himself to be ousted from it. The Tuscan, little accustomed to think of *rights*, and ever ready to sympathise with any manifestation of feeling or desire, tolerates any encroachment on them, and unscrupulously encroaches on those of others, expecting—not in vain—to be tolerated in turn.

It was not difficult, therefore, for Francesca and the three gentlemen with her, to make their way up the length of the nave into the transept. The bay-wreath carried by the former, moreover, sufficiently indicated to everybody in the crowd that she and her friends were among those more especially interested in the commemoration about to be celebrated, and that they had a function to perform at the upper end of the building. The majority of the crowd at the lower, or western end of the church, were naturally mere lookers-on, though almost all more or less warmly sympathisers in the business of the day; and they made way, not without a feeling and looks of mournful sympathy with the little group.

In the large open space of the transept in front of the wall on which the tablets were affixed, the crowd that had collected before them was composed almost wholly of those who had a special interest in the anniversary of a similar nature to that of Professor Varani and his party. There were fathers and mothers who had sent forth sons for the cause of Italy, who had come back no more. There were girls whose lives had been desolated and left empty by the untimely death of those for whose loss they could not be comforted. But the names of the beloved ones were there among the heroes on the roll of those whom Italy would remember as the proto-martyrs of her new liberty! And there was not a mourner there whose right to point evermore—he and his children after him—to the name of one among those who fought and fell at Curtatone, as one of their own, was not envied!

There did not appear to be any agents of the authorities in the church, either soldiers or police force. It seemed as if the paternal government had decided on allowing the people to mourn their dead, and say their prayer in peace. But a sort of curtain of coarse sail-cloth had been hung up before the bronze tablets, so as to hide them entirely from the people. Whether the authorities of the government had imagined that by thus hiding the object of the people's reverence and regard from their eyes, they would succeed in preventing all commemoration of the day; or whether, as is most likely, the intention was merely to irritate the people into some act which should form an excuse for violent interference on the part of the police, is uncertain. But if the object of the government was to arouse a vehement feeling of indignation among the Florentines, that object was most fully attained.

A great many wreaths, some of evergreens, some of flowers, had, nevertheless, been brought and reverently laid on the broad pavement beneath the tablets; and the bringers of them were kneeling in prayer in considerable numbers; and the outside crowd of those who stood around was hushed in sympathy with the mourners, when a sound of voices raised in anger was heard from the outskirts of the crowd around those who were kneeling before the bronze tablets, and in a moment or two afterwards the report of a pistol reechoed through the building. At the same moment, the cause of the disturbance was evident to those whose eyes had been turned towards the veiled tablets. Some daring hand, obeying the impulse of a heart that had been stirred by the dastardly outrage to greater anger than it could control, had suddenly and violently torn down the curtain, and given the venerated tablets with the honoured names inscribed on them to the eager eyes of the people. Of course, an immense movement of the crowd and violent confusion were the immediate consequences. The vast church was filled first with articulate cries and loud unanswered queries; and then, with inarticulate shrieks of frightened women. As usual, in such cases, it was impossible to ascertain, at the time or afterwards, who had fired the pistol; though it is probable that the fact was well known to the government agents. For it could hardly have been fired by any one of the people otherwise than at some individual of the public force. Now, no one of that body was killed in the church; and if any one had been fired on and not killed, he would have reported the fact.

Francesca started up from her knees and pressed close to the side of her husband, who had been standing immediately behind her. Her heroism seemed all to have vanished with her military trappings, or with the inspiration of the cause which had induced her to assume them; for she turned pale, and trembled as her husband threw his arm around her.

"It is coming, then!" Rinaldo said, with a cool, concentrated indignation; "I thought as much! The vile wretches cannot leave us in peace with our dead! The remembrance is too burning a shame to them even for them to endure!"

"Let us get out of the church if we can!" said Francesca; "see, the crowd is all in movement, and the priests have ceased the service."

"Nay! let us remain, and see what comes," said the Professor; "we have broken no law, not even any order of the police. Let us remain quiet! Do not let us increase the confusion and the rush by attempting to leave the church. We cannot be punished for quietly praying here!"

"But what do you suppose that it is?" asked Giulio; "what is happening, or going to happen?"

"The agents of the police, seeing that the people gave them no cause for interfering, are purposely giving rise to disturbance; insulting some man—some woman, more likely—till they succeed in provoking a show of resistance; then making arrests, and ordering the clearing of the church. Oh! I know the ways of them!"

"Then the quieter we are, the more we shall puzzle them!" said the Professor; "I vote for quietly remaining where we are!"

A good many of those who had been gathered in the transept in front of the tablets seemed inclined to adopt the Professor's tactics. But the great bulk of the crowd were pressing down the nave tumultuously towards the great western doors, anxious only to leave the church. From the slightly elevated vantage ground of the transept, those who remained there could look down on the sea of heads pressing forwards in terror and disorder down the nave of the church. The police had no longer any difficulty in declaring that "disturbance" had taken place. There was disturbance enough! But the *sbirri** had knowingly and intentionally caused it.

Suddenly, in the midst of the tumultuous rush

* The odious name of the despotic and irresponsible agents of the police power.

of the terrified and excited crowd towards the doors, while each man was asking his neighbour what the matter was, and nine-tenths of the surging mass of people could give no reasonable reply to the question—amid the shrieking of the women which filled the enormous and solemn spaces of the church with strange and unseemly echoes, a sound still more strange and unseemly in that place was heard; and the suspicions expressed by Rinaldo, that the government would be found to have taken means to interfere with the peaceful commemoration of the anniversary, were but too fully verified.

Not having dared, under the circumstances of the case, to take the strong and unprecedented measure of forbidding the survivors to celebrate a requiem in memory of their lost relatives, the Grand-Ducal authorities had determined to interrupt the peaceful ceremony. The sound, which, strange and revoltingly startling as it was in such a place, was well known enough to every ear in the crowd to be at once understood and interpreted aright, was the tramp of a body of soldiers, entering the church from the end of the northern transept.

It has been explained, that the communication between the church and the convent, and the cloisters, and sacristies, opens into the former at that point. It became evident, therefore, that it had been the predeterminate intention of the government to interrupt the funeral service, for the troops must have been placed in the convent over-night, since assuredly none had been introduced into it in the course of the morning. The priests (monks of the adjoining monastery) must have been aware of what was about to take place. But to all else in that crowded congregation the surprise was complete.

Tramp, tramp, tramp, they came, one file after another, through the sacristy door, till a great part of the transept was filled with soldiers. The priests, at the first interruption of the service, had of course vanished into their sacristy, or into the chancel hidden behind the high altar. Two bodies of soldiers were marched into the church, each under the command of its own officer—one of Grand-Ducal, and one of Austrian troops. The difference in the subsequent conduct of these two bodies was very remarkable; and it is painful to be obliged to record that this difference was all to the advantage of the Austrian!

Tramp! tramp! the automaton-like personification of brute force came on; and the men, at successive words of command, which rung out hideously beneath the rafters of that roof—(oh! if it could be imagined that the spirits of those, whose sepulchres make those desecrated walls sacred, were conscious of the scene!)—filing across the whole breadth of the church, formed in a double line along the top of the steps ascending from the nave and side-aisles to the transept, thus cutting off the multitude who were thronging towards the western doors from those who had remained in the neighbourhood of the spot where the tablets were affixed.

As soon as the men had been thus formed, or after the pause of a few moments, they began to advance down the nave and side-aisles, driving and forcing the retiring crowd before them, which was escaping into the *piazza* as fast as the capacity of the three great doors, and the eagerness of the alarmed people, would permit them to do so. Meantime the police force in uniform, and the *sbirri* in plain clothes, were busy making numerous arrests among those who had remained in the rear of the soldiers.

In a very few minutes the nave was entirely cleared; and the troops, following the people out through the western doors, again took up a position on the steps before the west front of the church, thus commanding from an elevation of some six or eight feet the large space of the Piazza Santa Croce.

In the next minute a discharge of fire-arms was heard by those who had remained at the upper end of the church!

"Good Heavens! they are firing on the people!" exclaimed Rinaldo. "Is it possible!"

"Firing over their heads to disperse the crowd, most likely!" said Giulio.

"If they are killing our brothers, we should be with them," cried the Professor, making, as he spoke, one huge ungainly stride in the direction of the nave. "We are the guilty ones," he continued, "for we were of those who rebelled against our dear friends here in the white coats at Curtatone!"

But Francesca sprung after him, and, clinging to his arm, cried, "No! no! you said it was best to remain here! What good can you do? You cannot leave me here!"

"Possibly the people, outraged beyond all bearing, have broken out into resistance!" said Giulio, who had been attentively listening to the sound which reached the spot where they were at the farther end of the long church. "I hear a few dropping musket-shots among the roar of voices; but they have not fired a second volley. I shall go! I must see what is going on!"

But, as he spoke, a couple of *sbirri* stepped up on

each side of him, and made signs to one of the *carabinieri** to take him in charge.

"Never mind!" he cried to his friends, as he was hurried off, "they can't hurt me! Only take care that some one of you come to see me. I must speak with you!"

There is a side-door in the southern wall of the church, a little below the transept, opening into the Via dei Malcontenti; and the police agents were hurrying away the persons they had arrested through this exit. Many arrests were made. Indeed, all those who had remained in the rear of the soldiers might have been arrested if the police agents had thought fit to do so. But they probably considered that too large a bag of game might be embarrassing to their masters, and contented themselves with driving the greater number of the people out of the church through the same door by which they carried off their captures.

Malatesta was one of the last arrested; and Francesca and her husband and brother found themselves free in the comparatively quiet Via dei Malcontenti.

Meantime, what had happened on the western steps of the church and on the *piazza* was simply this. As soon as the soldiers had been formed in

* The armed police are so called.

line on the top of the steps, and while the excited crowd were massed in the open space before and below them, the Italian soldiers fired a volley into the then harmless crowd. *Then* harmless, I say, because it is true, that in the *mêlée* and confusion in the church, while the crowd was rushing towards the great doors, some of the police agents who were mixed up with the crowd were roughly handled. A few of them had to go into hospital, and were treated by the medical men for contusions about the head, and bruises. There were no knife wounds, and *no pistol-shot wound.*

Whether the Italian officer who gave his men the order to fire on an unarmed and unresisting crowd of men, women, and children, did so in obedience to previous orders, or in the exercise of his own discretion, was not known. It is, however, certain that the Grand-Ducal government approved the act, when it had been done; for no inquiry was instituted, and no slightest censure passed on the officer who had done the deed.

The Austrian soldiers stood by the side of the Italian soldiers on the steps of the church. But while the latter were firing at their fellow-countrymen, the Austrian troops stood motionless!

Thus was consummated one of those deeds which live in the memory of a people long after much bad government of far more widely influential evil tendency has been forgotten. For many a year yet, even though the deed has received its punishment, and the author of it has it not in his power to do further evil, the black day of Santa Croce will be remembered in Tuscany. It was vividly remembered on the memorable 27th of April, 1859, and contributed its part towards the passing of the irreversible decree, which on that day deposed a dynasty.

For the time, however, the Grand-Ducal government had its triumph and gained its object. The offending bronze tablets were removed that very night from the wall! It seems hardly credible that a sovereign should have been guilty of ingratitude so base, and meanness so contemptible. It was so, however. The tablets, recording the names of those who had fallen in an expedition sent forth to fight for their country by the sovereign who was so anxious to forget the fact, were removed, lest they should give offence to the brave enemy, who felt a soldier-like admiration for the foe which had opposed him. They were taken down from their place on the sacred wall, and the Tuscans were bidden to forget all about those untoward events at Curtatone and Montanara.

But the Tuscans did not forget them. And

when the Grand-Duke was taken down from his place, the tablets were hunted out from the lumber-cellar in the fortress into which they had been thrown, and were restored to the spot where they may now once again be seen.

The first care of Rinaldo and his wife and the Professor, as soon as they found themselves free in the Via dei Malcontenti, was to hurry homewards to the house by the Porta Romana, for the purpose of reassuring the poor old mother left at home, who had in so many ways already felt the smart of the political ills of her country. The entire city was, of course, greatly agitated by the events which had taken place; and the wildest rumours, as to the number of the slain and wounded, were flying about the town. To make the best of their way homewards, however, it was desirable to avoid the Piazza Santa Croce, which, under ordinary circumstances, would have been the shortest way. For the troops, though no firing had taken place since the beginning of the disturbance, were still there under arms; and in the lower part of the *piazza*, and the small streets opening on to it, there were still considerable masses of the population, and a great agitation prevailed; and there seemed reason to doubt whether the atrocity of the provocation might not yet prove to be too much even for the quiet and unresisting habits of a Tuscan population, and lead to ulterior and more serious disturbances. But there was a crushing force of Austrian troops in the city, and any attempt at insurrection would have been madness. Slowly, therefore, and with deep but muttered imprecations on their government, the people by degrees retired to their homes, and "order reigned in Florence."

Rinaldo and his wife and brother-in-law, turning their backs on the *piazza*, and following the Via dei Malcontenti to its farther end at the city wall, passed thence by the remote and quiet Via delle Torricelle to the Lung' Arno, and so crossing the Ponte alle Grazie, gained the Oltr' Arno quarter of the city, and reached the Porta Romana in safety.

Hardly a word was exchanged between them till they came to the walls at the extremity of the Via dei Malcontenti. By that time the noise of voices and the tramping of troops had died away behind them, and the remote part of the city which they had reached was as quiet as if nothing out of the ordinary course of the usual rather sleepy Florentine life had been taking place within the walls.

"A nice sort of welcome Florence has given to our friend Giulio on his arrival," said Rinaldo, as they stopped to listen, standing in the road under the grey old wall. "To think of his coming here by mere chance this morning to tumble into such a business!"

"It is well, at all events, that it was he rather than either of you two that the *sbirri* laid hands on," said Francesca; "not," she added, "that I think little of any evil to *nostro buon* Giulio—on the contrary; but, as he said, they cannot hurt him; and it would have been a very different affair if either of you had fallen into their clutches."

"Oh, no! they'll let him out fast enough when they find out who and what he is," said the Professor; "nevertheless, I am sorry he was taken. I was very anxious to have a talk with him."

"I am glad they have taken him!" cried Rinaldo; "the miserable vermin will find themselves in the wrong box, arresting an officer in the Piedmontese service, and no reason to give for it! Perhaps it may lead to something!"

"Do not forget what he said about going to see him," said Francesca; "you must go to-morrow morning without fail, Rinaldo;—or perhaps you had better go, Pietro *mio*, as you say you want to speak to him. Or why not both of you go together?"

"You are settling it all very much at your ease, *cara mia!*" returned Rinaldo. "I wonder where you learnt your ideas of imprisonment for political causes? Not at Bologna, in Pope's-land, I should think. Giulio will be in the Murate* in an hour from this; and how, I should like to know, can either the Professor or I get leave to see him?"

"You don't mean to say that he will be kept in solitary confinement?" said Francesca, aghast.

"*Che! che!* It is only a preventive arrest!" said the Professor.

"No! they won't think of refusing to let him see anybody," rejoined Rinaldo; "but leave must be asked. And I question very much if either I or Pietro—old Curtatone men—would get leave. And it would be wiser not to ask it. No! I'll tell you what I am thinking. Giulio told me that his first business in Florence was to see his old friend Carlo Brancacci. Now, Brancacci, though a good fellow enough, is in with lots of the court party. His uncle is a chamberlain. Brancacci would have no difficulty in getting an order to see him. And his asking for it would be likely to do him as much good as our asking for it would do harm."

"You are right, Rinaldo! That will be the plan!" said Francesca.

"Ill try and find Brancacci this afternoon, as soon as I have seen *la madre, poverina!* He will get

* The principal state prison of Florence, formerly a celebrated convent.

the order the first thing in the morning, and be with him before noon."

And Rinaldo having succeeded, in the course of the afternoon, in finding the comfortable and jovial Carlo discussing the affair of the morning among a knot of gossips at the door of Doney's café, and having further succeeded in drawing him on one side, and communicating his tidings to him, to Carlo's infinite astonishment, that laughing philosopher, but firm friend, *was* with the prisoner by noon the following day, as Rinaldo had said.

END OF BOOK V.

BOOK VI.

THE MARCHESE MALATESTA.

CHAPTER I.

THE MARCHESE FLORIMOND AND CARLO BRANCACCI.

THE dawn of a new era of regeneration and national independence, which shone with so brief and so delusive a splendour in Italy in 1848, was, as most of us still well remember, very quickly overcast. All the bright hopes faded away, and the nation sank back once more into the deep ruts of its old ways and its old evils. All this is matter of history, and is one of the most interesting chapters in the history of modern Europe. But the observers of social changes, and of the effects produced on the every-day life of the masses of the people by the movement of great political events, found a curious subject of study in the social phenomena to which the sudden clearing and rapidly succeeding gloom of the political sky in Italy gave rise.

In the early months of 1848, when sovereigns, lay and ecclesiastic, were tossing their crowns and tiaras into the air, and crying "Hurrah for Italy!" liberalism was the fashion, and everybody was an out-and-out liberal, except the few whom honest and strong conviction, or equally strong interest, enlisted on what then appeared the losing side. When all that was changed, when the sovereigns declared that all they had been saying and doing was an error or a jest, and that it was now time to give over fooling, and return to work and sober sense, of course the prevailing political fashion changed too. Liberty caps were no longer the only wear! *Good* society, with surprising readiness, put on caps of quite another form, had a new set of phrases on the tip of its tongue, forgot all that court manners required it to forget, and swam as buoyantly in one direction as it had in the contrary one before the tide turned. After Novara all the world was dynastic, except those (they were not so few as the previous minority had been) who were liberals and progressists from real conviction and true patriotism.

Of course this rapid right-about evolution required greater agility, and was more conspicuous in those who had been running strongest in the contrary direction. There was, however, a large class of people in whom a certain change of tone could be observed, if you marked them closely, but in whom it was very slight; people with whom the tide did not run strongly in either direction; some in whom scarcely any tidal movement could have been detected when the tide was flowing, and in whom, therefore, proportionably little change could be observed when it ebbed. And it was curious to note that some of such persons were equally disliked and abused by the stronger partisans of either tone of feeling and opinion, while others were excused and tolerated, and liked by both sides.

Of this latter sort was Carlo Brancacci. In his old student days at Pisa, in 1848, he had certainly called himself, and thought himself, a liberal, and had been the associate and dear friend of earnest and thorough-going liberals. But none of his friends and connexions among the "black" party had then shown him the cold shoulder, or shaken their heads and called him a dangerous man. And now, when the set of the social currents carried him naturally and easily into "dynastic" associations and habitudes, none of his old friends greatly blamed him, and much less dreamed of considering him their enemy. He was so jolly, so good natured, so full of fun and laughter; he was growing so fat; he so utterly ignored all political differences between his intimates, and would throw his arm over the shoulder of an old friend, though he were a marked Curtatone man, just as affectionately in the midst of a group of frequenters of the court as he had ever done in student days at Pisa, that he was accepted as a friend in both camps, without being required to do duty as belonging to either. No man in Florence had so large an acquaintance among all classes; and all his acquaintance were his dear friends.

There was a certain similarity of character between him and his uncle, the Marchese Florimond. But Carlo's was the larger, kindlier, and more genial nature. The difference was, that the Marchese Florimond hated nobody; but Carlo Brancacci loved everybody.

On the afternoon of the day after the terrible and memorable scene in the church of Santa Croce—of the 30th of May, that is to say—Carlo Brancacci was sitting closeted with his uncle in his bedroom in the little Brancacci palace in the Via Larga. It was about four o'clock in the afternoon, and the Marchese Florimond had just arisen from his *siesta*. Carlo, after his visit to Malatesta in the prison of the Murate, had hurried home, sure that his uncle would be at that hour asleep in his own cool room with the *persiane* carefully closed, and that any one sufficiently ignorant of the Marchese's habits to present himself at his door at that hour, would be sent away with the solemnly pronounced declaration of the old servant, "*Il Signor Marchese dorme.*"

It made no part of Carlo's intention to wake his uncle, for he wished to find him in perfect good humour, and in charity with all men; which he well knew would not be the case if the Marchese Florimond's *siesta* on a warm May afternoon were brought to any other than its natural termination. Having waited, therefore, patiently till this moment arrived in the due course of nature, and at its wonted time, Carlo sent in to say that he wished to speak with his uncle, and would be obliged if the Marchese would give him half an hour before he went out.

The conference between them lasted much longer than the time named, and the Marchese Florimond was missed that day in the Cascine.

"And you saw the documents supporting this extraordinary story?" said the Marchese, after he and his nephew had been talking some little time together.

"Oh, yes! he has them all with him. There is no doubt at all about the matter. Besides, the proof has been accepted, and all put in train at Bologna," replied Carlo.

"It is a most extraordinary story—a strange fatality! And, *per Bacco!* the discovery comes just in the nick of time! Truly I think one may see the hand of Providence in it!" said the little Marchese, nodding his bewigged head up and down with a sort of pious sententiousness, which seemed meant to imply an admission that perhaps, after all, there was something in such notions, though a layman and a Marchese could not be expected to be very conversant with such matters.

"I don't know about the nick of time," rejoined Carlo; "I don't think, for my part, that they would have succeeded in making the little Contessina marry that *animalaccio** the Marchese Alfonso, if you mean that."

"I don't know! Girls have to marry the men chosen for them by their families, and, after a little more or less of kicking, do so every day; and are very contented wives afterwards. But, any way, it is fortunate that all this has come out before the Contessina was sent away to her convent at Palazzuolo! *Per Dio!* I should not like to go and live in a convent at Palazzuolo! It is horrible to think of it," said the Marchese, shuddering a little as he spoke. "She was to have left Florence the day after to-morrow, or next day at farthest. The Canonico Adalberto is not a man to joke with! *Per Dio!* he frightens me, that man. *Vuole cio' che vuole, il Canonico Adalberto!*"†

* The depreciatory form of *animale*; "that nasty little animal."
† "He will what he wills."

"Ay! I should think he was a difficult customer to deal with! But it will be all right now!" said Carlo.

"And I am glad, with all my heart, that it will be in time to prevent her from being sent away into exile again, poor little Contessina! I say again, it is in the nick of time!"

"And not a moment is to be lost, if all is to be put right before the day named for the departure of the Contessina," observed Carlo.

"No time to be lost, *davvero!*" said his uncle; "and how do you purpose proceeding, since it seems that while *nostro povero Giulio* remains in prison, the matter is all in your hands."

The Marchese Florimond's mode of speaking of Malatesta was a safe symptom that his fortunes were brightening. Though, like a good-natured uncle as he was, he had opened his house to his favourite nephew's friend, he had never called him "*nostro* Giulio" before.

"What a *disgrazia*," he continued, "that he should have been arrested just at such a moment. But those stupid *carabinieri* are always putting their hands on the wrong man! But that will easily be put to rights!"

"Oh, yes!" replied Carlo, "there will be no difficulty about that! The minister will soon make it all right. A mistake! very sorry! and there's an end of the matter! *Che diavolo!* do mistakes never happen!"

"But what do you mean to do in the first place, Carlo *mio*?—speak to the Canonico Adalberto?—lay all the circumstances before him?"

"Not just yet! No! my notion is to have everything a little more prepared first! And I wish that you should have all the credit of bringing the matter about, uncle!" said the judicious nephew. "You are the friend of the family! You are the Marchese Brancacci! I am a mere nobody. It will come naturally and properly from you. It will be a pleasure to you, too, to communicate to the Contessa Zenobia what we must all know she will be pleased to hear."

"Yes, indeed! *La povera buona* Zenobia! It has gone to her heart to use severity towards the Contessina! If it had not been for the Canonico, she would never have had the courage to do it!"

"And she will not be sorry, if I know anything of the Contessa Zenobia, to hear that that animal Alfonso's nose is to be put out of joint, eh, uncle?"

"Indeed you may say so! She can't endure the insignificant little wretch. *Per Bacco!* the Contessa Zenobia knows too well what a man should be like to have any toleration for such a creature!"

"I believe you!" rejoined Carlo, with a wink, which was intended solely for his own private satisfaction.

"And what step do you propose that I should take first?" asked the little Marchese, exceedingly well pleased that the prominent part of the business in hand should be assigned to him.

"The first thing to be done is to put right this unlucky accident of the arrest. The fact is, between ourselves, this lamentable affair at Santa Croce is a very bad business altogether. But that does not concern us! Of course they will be ready enough to let a Piedmontese subject alone, and be glad enough to be sure they will hear no more of it. And, really, there does not seem to have been the smallest ground for arresting Giulio."

"*Diamine!* * of course not! It was all a mistake—a blunder of those stupid *carabinieri.* The minister will be the first to see it in that light."

"Do not you think that you will be able to see him about it to-night, so as to have an order for Giulio's release sent the first thing in the morning?"

"I will try! I will do so if it is possible! But I *must* accompany the Contessa to the Pergola, you know!" said the little man, as if he was speaking of the most sacred duty that any man could be called upon to perform.

* A common exclamation of assent, including an expression of surprise that anybody could imagine the reverse.

"Possibly you might see him at the Pergola," suggested Carlo.

"It is possible! And then it would be all easy. But if not, I will be with him the very first thing to-morrow morning. Of course I must tell him the whole circumstances?"

"There will be no need to enter on any question of the marriage. It will be sufficient to say what will induce him to sign the order for Giulio's liberation."

"And about the Contessa? What am I to say to her?" asked the docile Marchese.

"Oh! best say nothing yet. Let us wait till we have all ready. I must see this strange Abbess, too, somehow or other, and I have not an idea yet where she is to be found, or how to get speech of her maternity when I do find her."

"Ah! that may be likely enough to turn out a more difficult matter than the other," said the Marchese, shaking his head. "I heard a talk of heresy, or some such matter. And though I thought that the Signor Canonico seemed more inclined to sneer at the thing than anything else, still those black cattle keep their affairs so close, and are so jealous of being meddled with, that I should not be surprised if you were to find it a very difficult matter to get any opportunity of speaking to her, at all events privately."

"I do not know that it is absolutely necessary to speak to her privately. There will be nothing to be said that can do any mischief if overheard, if it comes to that," said Carlo. "I suppose they may put some old nun to see all fair between me and the Abbess. I have no objection!"

"I do not quite understand what it is you have got to say to her," returned his uncle; "and in fact, the whole story is so strange and puzzling, that I don't half understand it yet. What has the Abbess to do in the matter?"

"Why simply this. Giulio has, for a very long time, been most anxious, poor dear fellow, to discover his mother. And now, of course, it is more than ever desirable to do so. It is clear that the poor woman, whoever she is, has been foully wronged; and if she is alive, and this side of the Alps, we will find her out."

"But what has the heretical Abbess of Montepulciano got to do with the matter, in Heaven's name?" reiterated the Marchese.

"Why, Giulio has reason to think that she knows something of his mother's whereabouts. It seems that she herself told the Contessina Stella as much, and she wrote it to Giulio. He had been to Montepulciano to look her up, and had come thence to Florence the very morning that he was so unluckily arrested."

"Of course she will be found if she is alive," said the Marchese. "Under the altered circumstances of the case there will be little difficulty, I should say, in tracing her. It was different before this extraordinary discovery. As things are now, I should not wonder if you found it more difficult to get an interview with this Abbess than to discover the lady by other means."

"I think I know how to set about it, however," replied his nephew.

"I am sure that is a great deal more than I do!" returned the senior. "I know nothing about the way those sort of people manage their affairs. But I should not be astonished if the Archbishop's Apparitor, or whatever they call it, or some such extraordinary animal, was your especial friend; for you have friends in all sorts of out-of-the-way holes and corners!"

"Nay, my friend is nothing very much out of the common ranks of mortality this time," replied Carlo, laughing. "My old comrade and fellow-student at Pisa, Rinaldo Palmieri, had a sister in a convent at Pistoia. It was a house of the same order as that in which the Contessina was placed at Montepulciano—the Ursulines. And it strikes me as very probable that she may be able to help me to the information I am in search of. I know she is now in Florence, at her mother's house. I know the old lady, too, for when Giulio passed his Carnival here, three years ago, I went there three or four times with him and the Contessina and Mademoiselle Zélie to see her, and give her an opportunity of thanking Giulio for having saved the life of a son of hers in an accident at Pisa—a poor lad who was killed afterwards at Curtatone."

"Ah! that was a bad job, that Curtatone affair! —a sad mistake!" said the Marchese, shaking his head with the air of a Burleigh.

"And see," rejoined his nephew, in a tone of mock sententiousness, attuned to that of his uncle's last remark—"see how sure one is to suffer for it if one does a good action. If Giulio had not saved Enrico Palmieri's life in the Cascine at Pisa, the boy would not have gone to be killed at Curtatone. And if he had not been killed at Curtatone, his name would not have been written on these bronze tablets, which seem likely to make as much noise in the world as Moses' Tables of the Commandments. And if poor Enrico's name had not been on the list, Giulio would not have gone to Santa Croce yesterday with the boy's relatives to commemorate his death, and, consequently, would not have been arrested. It is a most imprudent act to save anybody's life. One is responsible for all they do in the world afterwards!"

"*Gia! pur troppo!*"* ejaculated the Marchese Florimond, in all seriousness.

"Well, uncle! it is never too late to learn! You must take warning by this example!" said Carlo.

"Take warning yourself, *figliuolo mio!* As for me, you jump into the Arno while I am standing on the bank, and you will see whether I have the lesson still to learn," retorted the Marchese, who had a vague idea his nephew was quizzing him, and who, at all events, did not relish the phrase "too late," as applied to him.

"Joking apart, however, my dear uncle," said Carlo, returning to his business-like tone, "there is one other matter connected with this affair that it would be well to attend to before we separate."

"Anything I can do to put things straight in such a manner——"

"I was thinking about the Marchese Cesare Malatesta at Fermo——"

"Ay! *per Bacco!* I do not know what he will say to it! It is an awkward business for him! Very awkward, take it any way, and look at it how you will!" said the Marchese, with an air of puzzled perplexity.

"He must lie on his bed as he has made it," returned Carlo. "But all that is nothing to us, and

* "Ay! it is but too true."

we are not called upon to do anything that can be ground of offence to him. On the contrary, it will be a friendly act to give him immediate notice of the facts which have come to our knowledge."

"Certainly! certainly! It is what I would wish any gentleman to do to me in similar circumstances—Heaven forbid that I should ever come into such circumstances!"

"Well, what I was going to suggest was, that you should write to him at once," said Carlo.

"It will be a very difficult letter to write!" returned his uncle, uneasily. "Do you happen to know if his second wife is still living?"

"No! I know that she is not. He has been a widower many years. She died, I believe, soon after the birth of the Marchese Alfonso."

"That is all the better—much better. She was a Sampieri, was she not?" asked the Marchese, thoughtfully.

"Yes! a Contessa Cecilia Sampieri, also of Fermo, I believe."

"Oh! yes! The Sampieri of Fermo! a very, very well-known family—wealthy, influential, and much looked up to in that part of the country. There was a Cardinal of the name not so very long ago. If I remember right, there were brothers. I think the Contessa Cecilia had brothers. Do you happen to know if any one of them is still living?"

"No! I know nothing about the family at all! Why do you ask?" said Carlo, looking observantly at his uncle.

"Oh! nothing! mere curiosity! It is nothing to us in any way. Only you conceive——for the Marchese Cesare! The Sampieri are a very proud family!"

"Humph!" said Carlo, "we are not called upon to look at that side of the matter at all; all that must settle itself as it can. Now for the letter to the Marchese Cesare! I do not see that it need be a very difficult one to write. I think I should not go into the circumstances, but write such a letter as must bring him here to Florence. It will be, on the whole, far better—necessary indeed—that he should be here. Give me pen and ink and I will scratch the rough copy of a letter to be corrected and put in proper order by you. You understand that sort of thing so much better than I can be expected to do. There is nothing like being conversant with Courts and the practice of great affairs for giving one tact and skill in such matters."

Thus judiciously flattered, the Marchese Florimond submitted without any difficulty to have his letter written for him by his nephew; who sat down at his uncle's rarely used writing-table, and produced the following epistle:

"ILLUSTRISSIMO SIGNOR MARCHESE,—

"Although I have never had the pleasure of making your personal acquaintance, I have little doubt that my name is known to you, as having been for many years honoured by the intimate friendship and confidence of the Contessa Zenobia Altamari, between whose niece and ward, the Contessina Stella, and your son, the Marchese Alfonso, it is proposed to form an alliance, which must be alike honourable and advantageous to either family. Your lordship,* has doubtless no need to be told by me, that some little difficulty is often experienced in such affairs, before the inexperience of a young girl can be led to see the advantages which mark the choice that has been made for her by her family. We have had some slight difficulty of this kind to contend with in the present case. I am not aware whether the Marchese Alfonso may have thought it worth while to trouble your lordship with any such trifles; and, under all the circumstances, I have deemed it best to write the present letter without communicating with him upon the subject.

"The fact is, that the little difficulty has been complicated in this case by a very singular chance,

* The word in the original is "Vossignoria;" for which the phrase in the text is the only translation. But the mode of address is used indiscriminately in writing to any gentleman.

which has so arranged matters, that the cause of the Contessina Stella's unwillingness to fulfil at once the engagements made for her by her family, arises from a girlish preference previously conceived for no other than the Marchese Alfonso's half-brother, Signor Giulio Malatesta!—an excellent and estimable young man, to whom the family of the Contessina Stella would have most willingly accorded her hand, had his position been that of the Marchese Alfonso.—A curious trick of the jade Fortune! is it not, Signor Marchese?

"Nevertheless, we should doubtless have succeeded with a little patience in smoothing away all these minor difficulties, had it not been that quite recently some very extraordinary circumstances have come to light,—or perhaps it would be more correct to say,—some very extraordinary assertions have been made touching nearly the position and interests of the Marchese Alfonso. It would seem, as far as I have been able to learn, that these assertions or reports have taken their rise from the death-bed statements and confessions of a certain Marta Varani, who died recently at Bologna, and whose son, Dr. Pietro Varani, Professor of Materia Medica in the University of Pisa, is now in Florence. The nature of these assertions, affecting as they very materially do, not only the Marchese Alfonso, but yourself also, is such as, in my humble judgment, to require your immediate presence in Florence. And I trust, Signor Marchese, that you will be of opinion that I have acted judiciously for your interest in giving you the earliest possible intimation of a matter which may, unless it be at once set at rest, lead to very serious consequences.

"I am, *Illustrissimo Signor Marchese*, with sentiments of the most distinguished respect,

"Of your illustrious lordship,

"The most humble and most obedient servant,

"FLORIMOND BRANCACCI.

"Florence, May 30, 1851."

"There," said Carlo, "I think that will do the business; which is to bring him to Florence, without telling him more of the cards in our hand than need be. The word I have dropped about the old woman at Bologna will no doubt be enough to frighten him. And I am sure the letter is courteous enough. But you will know better than me all about that, and will add any graces to the style that it may require."

So the Marchese Florimond sat down at once, and copied the letter his nephew had written, word for word; as the young man knew very well that he would do.

He sealed it, however, without handing it to Carlo again, saying, as he did so:

"There, that will do, I think. I have just

touched it up a little. But the gist of it is what you proposed. But when the Marchese Cesare comes here, what then?"

"Oh! Giulio will be at liberty by that time; and they must meet. Of course it must come to that. But whether it will be better for some one else to make him acquainted first with the real state of the case, we shall see. I should have no objection in life to undertake the job of doing so myself. The meeting between him and old Professor Varani will be a queer one. But I suppose they will have to meet too!"

"*È un pasticcio di quelli?*"* said the Marchese, lifting up his out-turned palms, and nodding his head.

"Yes! a queer business enough!" agreed Carlo; "but we and our friends are all on the right side of the hedge. And now I will go and talk to my old friend Signora Palmieri, and see if I can find out what I want from her daughter. You will remember your promise, uncle, like a dear good uncle as you always are, and see the minister to-night, if possible; and if not, the first thing to-morrow morning?"

* "*Pasticcio*"—a pasty. A phrase very commonly used to signify an embroiled and thorny piece of business: "It is a hash of such a sort as——" may be the rendering of the Marchese's observation.

"Never fear! my mind is too full of the matter for there to be any chance of my forgetting it, I can tell you!" said the Marchese.

"And we understand one another? Not a word as yet to anybody else!"

"All right!"

"Shall I post your letter? I must pass the post-office in the *piazza*."

"Yes! take it! It is time for me to think about dressing!"

"And oh! uncle!" said Carlo, turning as he was leaving the room, "I shall be anxious to know if you have seen the minister. If I come home later than you, as is likely, in case you have succeeded, tell Beppo to put a sheet of paper—see, there is one ready, so that you can't forget it—on the table in my room. If you have not seen him, don't do so. In that way I shall know before I go to bed."

"Very good! I feel as if I was turning conspirator, with all these signals and understandings!"

And so the uncle and nephew parted.

CHAPTER II.

THE ARCHBISHOP'S CHANCERY.

WHEN Carlo came home late that night—for after his visit to Signora Palmieri, he had strolled into the Pergola, and having first duly made a little round of visits to a circle of fair friends in the boxes, had joined a knot of young men, who were lounging in the open space between the hindmost benches of the pit and the doors of it, and had consented to go with them, after the opera was over, to sup at the *Bottegone;**—when Carlo at last reached his room in the Via Larga, there was no sheet of paper on his table.

He had thought it likely that he might see his

* *Bottegone*—literally, big shop, from *bottega*, a shop. It is the nickname of a well-known café, at which suppers may be had during the "small hours."

uncle on duty in the Contessa Zenobia's box at the Pergola. But he did not reach the theatre till the last act of the opera; and the Contessa Zenobia had departed as soon as the ballet was over, which at Florence is given between the acts of the opera.

It was evident, however, from the absence of the signal agreed on, that the Marchese had failed to see the minister. He had been more successful himself, inasmuch as he *had* seen the persons he went to see. But he had not succeeded in obtaining the information he needed. The Signorina Teresa Palmieri had been able, however, to put him in the way of ascertaining the facts. But half a day at least would be thus lost—the first half of the morrow, which was the 31st of May! And Stella, as matters now stood, was to leave Florence, at the latest, as the Marchese Florimond had said, on the 2nd of June!

Carlo was of opinion that the various facts which he was preparing to bring to the knowledge of the several parties interested in them, would, when they were known, have the effect of cancelling the Contessina Stella's destined journey to Palazzuolo. And he was very anxious to be in time to do so. But the time was very short. And he began to think how he could cause the putting off of this terrible journey for a few days, without disclosing the secrets, of which he was the depositary, before the proper moment for doing so arrived. He determined, however, to take no steps to that end just yet; but to content himself with losing no time in prosecuting his inquiries.

With this view he was on foot early the next morning, notwithstanding his late supper overnight; and leaving a note to be given to his uncle as soon as he was stirring, reminding him of his promise to see the minister with a view to Giulio's release early that morning, he succeeded before mid-day in ascertaining that the late Abbess of the nunnery of Santa Filomena at Montepulciano was now in a convent about three miles from Florence, in the direction of Sesto, and that an order from the Archbishop of Florence was requisite in order to be permitted to see her.

After a short debate with himself whether he should induce his uncle to make an application to the Archbishop for the required permission, or should ask him to give him, or procure for him, a letter of recommendation to that magnate, the consideration of the pressure of time decided him to take a more direct course. It was already too late for him to find the Marchese at home, especially as he had promised to go out early for the purpose of seeing the minister. He could not tell where he would be likely to fall in with him before the evening. The whole day would thus have been lost. He determined, therefore, to go at once to the Archbishop himself, trusting to the recommendation of his name, and the decidedly "well-affected" reputation connected with it.

Carlo's notion was that he would go to the Archbishop's door, ask if he was at home, and send in his card, desiring to see Monsignore!—drawing a very erroneous and delusive analogy between the supposed habits of Archbishops and those of ordinary mortals. Carlo, though he had seen the Archbishop in the flesh, sitting with a great gold chain and cross round his neck, and a chaplain opposite to him, in a huge rickety old-fashioned carriage with two long-tailed blacks in front, and two seedy-looking cocked-hatted footmen behind; and might even have come within blessing range of his fingers (supposing the rays of benediction from episcopal forefingers to be subjected to laws at all analogous to those of the rays of light); had never spoken to any higher ecclesiastical dignitary than the Canon Adalberto Altamari. Not being, however, of those natures which are overpoweringly awed by the exteriors of human greatness, he had a very imperfect conception of the majesty which doth hedge an Archbishop, and had no idea that there was any difficulty in coming face to face with him.

He knew well—who in Florence does not?—the queer, ancient-looking ramshackle old pile of building to the west of the Baptistery, which is the Archbishop's palace; but he had never been inside it. By coasting, however, round those parts of the amorphous dust-encrusted old building, which front the Piazza di San Giovanni, and the Via dei Marignolli, he found in an obscure little lane called the Via dei Suchiellinai, or "Street of the little gimlet-makers," a low-browed archway, which gave entrance into an interior court, by a slight descent —the measure of the rise which in the lapse of centuries the progress of civil life had caused in the surrounding thoroughfares, while the Archbishop's dwelling, as changeless as himself, had remained characteristically at its ancient level.

There was a specially forlorn, mouldy, and silent air of quietude about this court, which contrasted strongly with the bustling life of the busiest part of the city outside it. The greatest part of it was in deep shade, and had that dank look, and those green shades about its stones, which indicate perpetual exclusion of the sunshine. One corner of the square space, however, was illuminated by a slanting ray, the habitual presence of which had imparted a quite different tone to the colouring of the walls of that part of the building. And on a stone bench in this privileged corner sat an old servant in the reddish chocolate-coloured episcopal livery, with the usual lavish abundance of coarse worsted lace on all the seams.

The servants of the Roman Catholic hierarchy, in Italy at least, are always remarkably shabby and dirty—I know not why, unless, perhaps, it be for the want of a mistress's eye to take note of such matters—and the specimen in question was no exception to the rule. His abundantly-laced livery looked as if it had been slept in for years; and the wearer looked as if he were then sleeping in it. He stretched himself and yawned, but without rising from his seat in the sunshine, as Carlo came up to him. Nor was he startled into the exertion of speaking even by the unprecedented monstrosity of that jaunty young gentleman's demand, whether the Archbishop was at home? It *did* make him open his eyes, and stare at the applicant; but he vouchsafed no other reply than a listless movement of his hand towards a small half-glazed door, inside a strong outer door which was standing open in another corner of the court.

Obeying this silent indication as the only course before him, he opened the glazed door, and found himself in a small, dark, and very mouldy-looking room, and in the presence of two still more mouldy-looking individuals, belonging to that peculiar class which has been described in the first book of this narrative, who were sitting behind a table covered with oil-cloth, and encircled by a curtain of green calico, in such sort that the lower part of the persons of those sitting behind the table were invisible. On it were writing materials, one or two stamps, and materials for making an impression of them on paper in red or black. The men were, however, doing nothing;—apparently not even talking to each other. Against the wall opposite to them, under the window, which was so high as to be above the head of a man, there were two or three rush-bottomed chairs; and these were the only other things in the room besides the tables, and the men sitting behind them.

The two men stared at him with lacklustre eyes, without speaking, when he entered; and stared still more, when he repeated his demand for the Archbishop. After motioning him to sit on one of the chairs against the wall, they proceeded leisurely to discuss in an under tone the nature of a case evidently altogether unprecedented in their experience; and at last one of them, with visible reluctance, dragged himself from his chair and sauntered into an inner room, the door of which he presently held open, and signed to Carlo to enter.

There, in a somewhat better furnished room, sat, also behind a table similarly covered and similarly curtained round its legs, a man of a higher grade of that same class of hybrid lay-clerical functionaries. He somewhat more courteously begged Carlo to be seated, and asked him his business, and his "*casato*." *

Carlo showed his card (which evidently produced an immediate impression), and said that he wished to speak to the Archbishop on business of a very particular and urgent description.

"It is not—ahem—usual, Signor Marchese—(Carlo, as *dei* Marchesi Brancacci, had a right to the title)—for the Archbishop to receive—ahem—applicants without previous appointment, and without knowing the nature of the business they wish to speak on. But I have no doubt that his reverence the Archbishop's chaplain would see *you*—(with a bow and a marked emphasis on the word)—and you would probably find that it would serve your purpose as well as seeing the Archbishop himself."

Carlo expressed his willingness to confide his business to the ear of the chaplain, and the official,

* A phrase which simply means, what was his name? But it is a more courteous mode of putting that question; and may be Englished by "To what family do you belong?" The nature of the flattery intended to be conveyed originally is evident. But this, like all other forms of Italian courtesy, from having been at first a special flattery addressed to the great, then a recognised form proper in speaking to persons of station, has come to the universal mode of asking any man's name.

who had recommended that course, taking with him Brancacci's card, left him for a few minutes, and then came back, saying that the chaplain would see him.

The man who received him in a small but comfortably furnished snuggery, occupying a *mezzanino** in the palace, and reached from the abovementioned offices on the ground floor by a small secret stair, was a very different sort of individual from that Archbishop's chaplain who had bullied poor Pietro Varani at the memorable interview with the Cardinal after the clandestine marriage. This was a young man, not many years Carlo's senior, and dressed as elegantly as the strict rules of ecclesiastical costume would permit. And within those limits there was plenty of room for a considerable display of clerical dandyism. The knee and shoe buckles were gilt, and small. The stockings, perfectly well drawn over the well-shaped leg, were of silk instead of worsted. The shoe was well cut and well fitting; the professional collar scrupulously clean, the straight-cut frock-coat of fine glossy cloth, and admirably fitting the waist and shoulders; and he wore one or two rings of value on the taper fingers of an exquisitely white hand.

* A mezzanino is the same thing as what the French call an "entresol."

He rose as Carlo entered the room, and courteously inviting him to take a seat, waited the opening of his business with a smile on his face, which seemed to ask what on earth such an one as Carlo could want with him.

"The fact is, your reverence," said he, encouraged by the appearance and manner of his interlocutor to speak more openly than he would otherwise have been inclined to do—"the fact is, that in my ignorance of all such matters, I imagined that I could see the Archbishop, and ask him at once the favour I desire, and tell him the motives of my asking it. It seems that such is not the case."

"Why, no!" said the chaplain, relaxing into a still more friendly smile; "it would never do, you see. The business to be transacted is too much in quantity, and in quality rarely so agreeable as the present"—(with a courteous bow and an extra smile). "It is usually my duty to attend, in the first instance, to the applications of those who have business with Monsignore. In what can I serve you?"

"Well!" said Carlo, "the application I wished to make is a strange one; and to explain and show a reason for it, it is necessary to speak of a portion of the private family history of a valued friend of mine. I felt that I might safely confide this to the ears of the Archbishop. And I doubt not that it may be equally trusted to the discretion of your reverence."

"My dear Signor Marchese," said the young chaplain, nodding his head, "we have to become the depositaries of a great many more strange secrets than you may think for. The honour of many a family is in our keeping—and is, I believe, perfectly safe. In any case, I think I may venture to say that you may confide to me what you had made up your mind to tell to the Archbishop."

"No doubt! no doubt!" said Carlo; "and I shall be most happy if you will kindly give me your advice in the matter. Your reverence is doubtless aware of the case of a Superior of a convent of Ursuline nuns at Montepulciano, who has been transferred to Florence, under accusations of heresy, or misconduct of some sort?"

"Oh! yes! I know that there is such a case! The Mother Abbess of Santa Filomena! She has been sent to a convent out towards Sesto. Some convent quarrel! It is all stuff and nonsense about heresy, you know," said the chaplain, taking that sort of tone which Roman Catholic ecclesiastics of a certain class are apt to adopt when speaking with educated men of the world, and which seems to imply an understood admission that between themselves all these professional matters of theirs are, of course, absurd puerilities, but are parts of a comedy necessary to be acted before the eyes of the vulgar;—"all mere silly trash about heresy, or any such big words," said the chaplain; "some stupid provincial quarrel or other! But it will be probably necessary to remove the Abbess from her position, and place her in some other convent. There will be no quieting the silly women else! It is a pity that the whole lot of them can't be condemned to a twelvemonth of absolute silence!" added the chaplain, with a laugh.

"In truth, your reverence is in the right of it," rejoined Carlo, laughing; "but it is not about the Abbess that I wished to speak at present. The fact is, that a lady with whom the Marchese Malatesta formed a *liaison* in early life before his marriage, and who was, in all probability, placed in some convent by the care of the late Cardinal, the present Marchese's uncle, has been lost sight of for many years. The lady in question had a child, who was, during the Cardinal's life, supported and educated by his care; and it is now desired, if possible, to discover whether the mother is still alive or not. And, curiously enough, it seems that this Abbess, hearing, Heaven knows how! of these particulars, has communicated to some of the family that she can give some information on the subject of this missing lady. Now, all I want, Signor Abate, is a permission to speak with the Abbess on the subject on behalf and as a friend of the family."

It will be observed that Carlo slyly told his story so as to leave on the chaplain's mind the impression that the information sought was desired by the magnates of the family, and not merely by the outcast son of the bond-woman. For he knew enough of the ways of dignified churchmen to be aware that any assistance asked by such an one towards the discovery of a fact which "the family" wished to conceal would have small chance of being granted.

The chaplain, however, supposing that he was obliging the Marchese Malatesta, and quite re-assured by the name, and connexions, and social position of Brancacci, said:

"Oh, there will be no difficulty about that! And I should not be a bit surprised if the old lady were able to help you in your search. Nuns are terrible gossips. Bless you! they know all sorts of things;—pick up facts as magpies do missing trifles, and hide them away as carefully."

"Can your reverence complete your kindness by procuring me the order at once?" asked Carlo.

"I dare say I can," replied the obliging chaplain.

"I can write it in two minutes. But it must have the Archbishop's signature. I dare say I can get him to sign it at once, though his time for doing such things is an earlier hour of the morning. But he is very kind, and if I tell him that time is urgent——"

"I should be so much obliged to you!" said Carlo, eagerly, in dismay at the idea of losing another four-and-twenty hours. If he had known how many applicants, unfortunate enough to have any business to transact with that Archiepiscopal "Chancery," are compelled to lose, not hours or days, but weeks and months, in cases when days are of greater importance than they were to him, how many weary hours are passed sitting on those miserable chairs against the dank wall of that miserable outer office, to be ended by an apparently altogether arbitrary and meaningless intimation that the hapless and despairing suitors "must return again another day," he would have been more thankful for the chaplain's alacrity, or have estimated more highly the advantages of being "L'illustrissimo Signor Carlo dei Marchesi Brancacci."

The chaplain wrote the order, as he had said, in two minutes; and then, desiring his visitor to wait a few moments, left the room by a different door from that opening on the secret stair, by which Carlo had reached it, and in a very short time brought back the required signature.

"There! Signor Marchese; it is all right. By-the-by," added the chaplain, "you know, of course—or rather," he added, with a laugh and a look that approached curiously near to a wink without absolutely being one, "of course you *don't* know enough of the ways of nunneries to be aware, that one of the sisterhood of the house will have to be present at your interview with the Abbess. But there are two ways of being present at an interview. And I will write a line to the Superior of the house, which will prevent you from being annoyed by any eaves-dropping. I am glad I thought of it."

Carlo reiterated his acknowledgments; and the chaplain scribbled a little note to the Superior, which he enclosed in a huge square envelope, and sealed with a huge official seal.

"I have written the order generally," added the chaplain, "so that if you find it necessary to repeat your visit, you can do so without any fresh application here. But perhaps you will let me hear the upshot of the business, for I take an interest in it. The routine of our ordinary affairs here is sufficiently uninteresting——"

Carlo promised that he would return and tell the obliging chaplain the whole story as soon as he became acquainted with it; thinking it natural enough that curiosity should be excited by so strange a romance, and never dreaming that the reverend gentleman's only real motive was the cultivation of an acquaintance with himself.

Again thanking the chaplain for his kindness, he was dismissed by him through a door which led him by two or three other rooms to the main staircase of the palace; so that he had not to return through the miserable offices on the ground floor.

"When next you give me the pleasure of seeing you," said the chaplain, as he parted from him, "ask for me by name, and you will be shown in by this road; the other is for other purposes. *Addio*, Signor Marchese!"

Carlo lost not a minute, as soon as he was outside of the Archiepiscopal palace, in jumping into a *fiacre*, and telling the driver to make the best of his way out of the Porta di Prato, and along the road towards Sesto.

CHAPTER III.

CARLO BRANCACCI AND THE ABBESS.

Carlo may be excused for not giving all the attention it deserved to the exceeding beauty of the drive, about half the distance to Sesto—the sixth milestone on the road to the little city of Prato—which took him to the convent he was in quest of. The road lying first along the lowest slopes of the villa-studded hill of Fiesole, and then creeping close at the foot of the sterner, but still beautiful, Monte Morello, has beauties of no ordinary kind. "Monte Morello, the dark mountain," as the Florentines call it, is no longer such when the rays of an afternoon Italian sun are lighting up the folds in its huge flank. It is then a purple—a rose-coloured—a violet-coloured—an amber mountain; for a hazy bloom of all these colours melting into each other lies upon it. The road to Sesto is just sufficiently raised above the irrigated flat of the broad and fertile valley to show the whole of its variegated green surface to the traveller, and to give him the panorama of the Cascine woods, and the darker sides and tops of the lower range of hills, which shut in the valley of the Arno to the southward.

The Italians are in general very much less insensible to landscape beauty than the French, especially to the charm of colour in scenery; and at another time Carlo would not have failed to appreciate the beauties of his afternoon drive. But he was, on the occasion in question, too anxious about his coming interview with the Abbess to have any thoughts for the scene around him. He was anxious on his friend's account about the result of his quest; but he was also—which was strange for Carlo Brancacci, and very unlike his usual self—a little nervous about his interview. He had never spoken with, or even seen an Abbess in his life. He was conscious of being wholly ignorant of the proper mode of addressing her, and behaving towards her. His embarrassment was increased by the knowledge that she was an Abbess under a cloud. For the first time in his life he felt shy and diffident. And he spent the entire time during which his little journey lasted in trying to figure to himself what the Abbess would say to him, and what he should say in return.

A little less than an hour sufficed to bring him to the door of the convent—a little building of very humble pretensions attached to a picturesquely-situated church, the raised terrace on the hill-side in front of which, shaded by a group of magnificent cypresses, made it a marked object, as seen from the valley below. A couple of old women were sunning themselves in the afternoon warmth on this exquisitely situated little terrace in front of the open door of the church; the lamp at the farther end of which, burning before the altar, glimmered in contrast with the glory of heaven's light outside, like the pale lamp in the hand of a miner, seen at the far end of a long subterranean gallery. The two old crones, who were attracted to the spot probably by some half unconscious sensation of the beauty of it, mingled with an equally indefinite idea that some advantage of a spiritual kind accrued to them from passing their time in the vicinity of the open church, were roused from their half-sleep to wide-awake astonishment at the extraordinary sight of a carriage from the city drawing up at the door of that remote little religious house; and forthwith came hobbling up to beg of the stranger. The old women wero not professional mendicants, and had not come there with the slightest intention of begging; where indeed they might have come every day in the year without ever seeing a soul of whom they would have dreamed of asking alms. But a Tuscan peasant, in the neighbourhood of Florence especially, is ever unhappily ready to assume the character of a beggar at the shortest notice, on the sight of a stranger. And Carlo, like a genuine Tuscan of the better class, put an infinitesimal coin into the hand of each—a fraction of a farthing—with which they hobbled off perfectly contented.

It seemed to Carlo an immense time after he had pulled the little iron ring attached to a chain, which passed through a door of the building, niched into a corner between it and the contiguous church, before any notice was taken of his summons. Yet he had pulled it, not as an Englishman pulls a bell, with one single pull, but as Tuscans are wont to do, with three or four pulls one after the other; not because they are impatient, but because they deem such an application of force necessary to cause a bell to ring.

At last, a little door about five inches square, cut in the panel of the large door was opened, and disclosed a little iron grating behind it—for the aperture of five inches square was deemed, Heaven only knows why! too large to be left wholly unprotected. And behind the grating a pair of black eyes under shaggy grey eyebrows, surmounted by a snow-white hood—(nuns are generally as clean as monks are the reverse)—gleamed through the grating, and a harsh voice demanded the visitor's business.

Carlo managing so to fold the two papers of which he was the bearer—the Archbishop's order, and the chaplain's letter to the Superior—as to enable him to thrust them between the bars of the grating, requested that they might be given to the head of the house. And the old portress, having eyed him with extreme curiosity and surprise, bade him wait a few minutes where he was, and she would bring him an answer.

Again Carlo's undisciplined patience was somewhat severely tried, and he began to imagine that there must be something informal or wrong in some way about the order he had presented. At last, however, he heard a withdrawing of bolts on the inner side of the door, which was presently opened, and he was bidden by the same harsh voice which had before spoken to him to enter and follow her.

She carefully closed, locked, and re-bolted the small but massive round-headed door behind him; and then preceded him along a narrow passage between spotless white-washed walls, tinkling from time to time a little hand-bell which she carried, in order to warn the inmates of the house to keep themselves out of the way and out of the sight of the male stranger. She opened a door at the farther end of the passage, and ushered him into a cheerful-looking, but almost unfurnished square room, of rather large size. It was cheerful by reason of two large windows, which opened on a neat and well-kept garden, full of sunshine and bright flowers. But within, there was little enough that was agreeable to the eyes. The walls were white-washed like those of the passage, and were hung with some half dozen coloured engravings of the vilest description in mean frames, representing scenes from the life of the Virgin Mary. Around these bare-looking walls were ranged a few rush-bottomed chairs, and in the middle of the room was a plain square deal table, with an inkstand, a pen, and a sand dish on it. There was no other article in the room; no fire-place; and the floor was of naked, but perfectly clean-swept bricks.

Carlo approached one of the windows, and regaled his eye with the sunny peacfulness of the pretty scene beneath it. But as before five minutes had elapsed he had tired of the occupation, and was again impatient, it seems probable enough that those whose only outlook for long years was this same peaceful garden, might cease to appreciate the poetry of the scene, and become not a little sick of the peacefulness of it.

At last the door opened and two figures entered. It was impossible for Carlo to doubt for an instant which of the two was the Abbess, even if in return for his grave obeisance the taller and younger woman had not given him the formal benedictory finger-flourish, which indicated that she had not yet at least been deposed from her ecclesiastical rank. The other woman, the older of the two, immediately took a chair, and placing it near the door by which they had entered, rested her bent knees against the front part of the seat, and bending down her face and head over the back of it, became to all appearance entirely immersed in the telling of her beads.

The Abbess, stepping across the room not without some stateliness of manner to the window at the side farthest from the door, motioned to Carlo to place chairs close to it.

"*Reverenda Madre*," said Carlo, who remained standing till the Abbess made a sign to him to be seated; "*Reverenda Madre*, I am here as the particular and intimate friend of Signor Giulio Malatesta." (The Abbess gave a slight start; and any one who had been more observant of the person he was talking with, and less occupied with thinking of what he had to say himself than Carlo, would have noticed that her pale cheek was overspread for a minute by a delicate flush.) "We were comrades at Pisa, and—and—I am commissioned—that is to say, he desires me to tell your maternity, that—in short, that you can say to me freely anything that concerns him."

"May I ask of you, my son, why, if it is the wish of Signor Giulio Malatesta to communicate with me, he prefers to send a friend rather than to come hither himself?" replied the Abbess, speaking in a low and singularly sweet tone of voice.

"Signora," said Carlo—"pardon me, *mia Madre*, I would say; that is explained more easily than satisfactorily. It is possible that your maternity may have heard, that on the occasion of the anniversary of the battle of Curtatone, there was some difficulty between the police and the people. Giulio, who had arrived in Florence only that morning, was unfortunately arrested, together with several others, in the church of Santa Croce. He was guilty of no offence against the government, and will, doubtless, very shortly be set at liberty. Other friends are busy in taking care that such shall be the case. But, in the mean time, he is unable to wait on your maternity."

"Perhaps you are, at least in some degree, acquainted with the nature of the subject on which he wished to speak with me?" said the Abbess, in the same low, sweet tones.

"Oh, yes!" returned Carlo, beginning to feel

more at his ease, and speaking more in his natural manner; "I know all about it. I may say, I believe, that Giulio honours me with his entire confidence."

The Abbess looked up at him for an instant with more attention than she had yet bestowed on him, and then with a little gracious bow, awaited his further explanations.

"The fact is," continued Carlo, "that some time since, it was intimated to my friend,"—and here Carlo became again embarrassed, not knowing how far he might be doing mischief by compromising Stella as the author of the "intimation," "in a letter from—from a friend;" he went on hesitating—

—"Yes!" interrupted the Abbess, "by a letter from the Contessina Stella Altamari——"

"Exactly so, your maternity!" continued Carlo, with a bow and a smile, and now feeling that he was on safe ground; "from the Contessina Stella Altamari; it was intimated to him in a letter from the Contessina Stella, that it was very probable that your maternity might be able to afford my friend Malatesta important information regarding a matter that has long been one of great anxiety to him—the discovery of his mother. May I ask your maternity," he continued, after a pause, "if you are aware of the circumstances of my friend Malatesta's birth?"

"I am not unacquainted with those circumstances," replied the Abbess, speaking in a still lower tone than before, and casting down her eyes to the floor.

"You will be aware, then," continued Carlo, "that it is the dearest wish of Giulio's heart to find the unfortunate mother whom he lost in infancy?"

"Nay, Signore!" said the Abbess, forgetting in her emotion, and in the extra-conventual nature of the subject, the mode of address prescribed by the ecclesiastical etiquette of her position, "my knowledge of the circumstances of his birth does not include any knowledge of his present feelings and wishes."

"Surely," said Carlo, with some surprise in his voice, "the one follows from the other. Of course he is very anxious,—or whether it is of course or not, he *is* very anxious to find his mother,—*very* anxious; it is the great anxiety of his life."

"Are you aware, Signore, since you have, as you say, been so long and so intimately his friend, whether he has long felt the anxiety you speak of?" said the Abbess, still speaking hardly above a whisper, and, as it seemed, Carlo fancied with surprise, almost tremulously.

"Unquestionably as long as I have known him, it has been his great desire. But since his position has become changed, since, as I may say, he *has* a position, and a good one in the world, he is naturally still more desirous than ever to find his mother, to whom he might now offer a support and comfort, which, before he had made a place for himself in the world, he could not have offered to her."

"It is, however, a long time—several months—since the communication you have alluded to was made to him," said the Abbess, still not looking up from the floor.

"Yes! In the first place it seems not to have reached him till a long time after it was written. And then business of a very important nature,—the upshot of which, I may say, makes it more desirable than ever that he should discover his mother,—required his immediate presence in the south of France."

The Abbess here lifted her eyes for an instant, and shot one sharp inquiring glance into Carlo's face; but finding nothing there but calm business-like attention to what he was saying, she dropped her eyes again to the floor while he continued.

"As soon as ever he returned from that journey, he hastened to Montepulciano in the hope of finding your maternity there. Failing in that hope he followed you to Florence, where, within a few hours of his arrival, he was unfortunately arrested and thrown into prison, as I have already said;

and being thus incapacitated from following up the inquiry he has so much at heart himself, his first thought was to depute me to do so for him. I, on my part, may certainly claim to have lost no time. I took immediate steps to ascertain the place of your maternity's present residence. Having succeeded in that, I went at once to the chaplain of the Archbishop, and obtained from him the order—dated not two hours ago—which has procured for me the advantage of the present interview."

"I have every reason to be grateful to you, Signore, for your zealous activity," murmured the Abbess.

"Say, rather, that Giulio may be satisfied with my care for his interests," replied Carlo somewhat surprised; "though doubtless," he added, "it will be a gratification to your maternity to contribute to a result which will make the happiness of a mother and her son."

"But that is just the point which demands mature and serious consideration," said the Abbess, looking up, and speaking with more decision and strength of voice than she had done previously.

"How so?" said Carlo in a voice of surprise. "What is the point to which your maternity refers?"

"*Would* it be a result contributing to the happiness of your friend, if we were to succeed in finding this lost mother? I am glad, Signore, to have an opportunity of speaking with a judicious and tried friend of Signore Malatesta on this point before communicating on the subject with him himself. I put it to you, as his friend, and as a man knowing more of the world and its ways than a poor recluse can pretend to do, whether it would be for the advantage of Signore Giulio Malatesta to discover a mother lost under such circumstances. I put it to your serious consideration, not only the question whether it would be well, as regards his position in the world, to find a mother who must bring disgrace with her when found——"

"But allow me to observe——" said Carlo.

"Excuse me, Signore," interrupted the Abbess, in her turn, with a courteous but slightly authoritative wave of her slight and elegant white hand; "excuse me, if I beg you to allow me to finish what I was saying. I have put the questions, I was putting to you, very earnestly before myself—a poor recluse, necessarily very ignorant of the world, and of the motives and feelings that rule men in it—and I shall be truly glad to have the mature opinion of a man of the world, and a devoted friend of Signore Malatesta on the subject. I was about to ask of your judgment, whether it would be advantageous to Giulio Malatesta to discover a mother who must bring disgrace with her——"

Carlo again opened his mouth to speak, but remained silent in obedience to a gesture of the Abbess.

—"And further, whether in a strictly moral point of view it would be good for him to make such a discovery;—whether the good feeling towards that unknown mother, with which he is now animated, could be trusted to continue towards a mother known only as a source of pain and trouble and disgrace;—whether it might not be safer for the happiness, and even for the moral nature of both these persons, that they should remain unknown to each other? I desire, I say, your best attention and well-considered opinion on these points. We must take care, in such a case as this, that we do not bring about evil instead of good."

"But had not these considerations occurred to, and been decided by your maternity, before you communicated in the first instance to my friend the hopes you held out to him," asked Carlo.

"Doubtless they had occurred to me—*pur troppo!*" said the Abbess with a deep sigh. "When you have reached my years, my son, you will probably be aware that when one doubts greatly, one may be led to take a step towards acting, in one sense, without being definitively and satisfactorily convinced that the opposite may not be after all the wisest. I have doubted *very* greatly in this matter. I have no objection to tell you that the communication made to Signor Malatesta was made very much in accordance with the urgent desire of the lady who wrote to him, as you have mentioned. I had the advantage of her opinion on the subject—the opinion of a pure and unsullied heart at all events, if not of a much experienced head, and of one as devotedly the friend of Signor Malatesta as yourself. And now I desire, as I have said, to have the benefit of your counsel on a point which requires so much circumspection."

"Your maternity does my poor judgment far too much honour to imagine that it is worth the having," returned Carlo; "I have never had the happiness of knowing a mother myself! But my notion would be all for finding her if she was above ground, let her be who she might, and what she might! And that is the feeling of Giulio. That would be his feeling, let what would be his position, whether he was the Marchese Malatesta with a big estate, or a poor student at Pisa with nothing at all, or a soldier of fortune with a good sword and good prospects, as he is now! In any case it is a sorrow and a bitterness to him to think that there is somewhere a poor mother with no son's love to comfort her! Lord bless you—I beg your maternity's pardon," said Carlo, thinking that such a colloquialism might very likely sound improper to ecclesiastical ears,—"I only meant to say that I know very well what he feels; he wants to have a mother's love, and to give a mother his love. And as to *her* share in the matter, I can only say that if you knew Giulio as I know him, you would feel it to be such a cruelty as you would not wish to be guilty of, to stand in the way of her recovering such a son! Be she who she may, or what she may, she may be proud and thankful to be the mother of Giulio! But——" continued Carlo, in a voice of *crescendo* eagerness, —and then he suddenly stopped.

"But what?" asked the Abbess, looking up quickly, with a sort of alarmed expression in her eye.

"But——I was going to say——I was thinking," stammered Carlo, evidently doubtful and puzzled, "I was going to tell your maternity, in short, that certain facts, which have recently come to my friend's knowledge are such as——are of a nature to make it far more desirable than ever——far more desirable than it was before, that Giulio should succeed in discovering his mother."

"Indeed!" said the Abbess, looking up with a

puzzled expression. "May I ask, Signore, if you are acquainted with the nature of the circumstances you allude to?"

Carlo paused for awhile before answering her, plunged apparently in anxious thought.

"Frankly, then, *Madre mia*," he said at length, "I *do* know all about the circumstances in question. And my hesitation was caused by doubting whether I ought to tell them to you, or to leave them to be told by Giulio himself. I think the last will be best. He will, I trust and believe, be at liberty very soon; and perhaps I shall act more rightly in adhering strictly to the terms of my commission, which was to entreat your maternity to communicate to me the information you may have it in your power to bestow. Doubtless Giulio will do himself the honour of waiting on you, and can then act as he may think fit about his own secrets; they are family secrets of great importance. But I may say that the facts to which I am alluding make it very clearly and unmistakably far more desirable than ever, as I have said already, that the missing lady should be found. I may add that the facts which have recently been brought to light are of a nature entirely favourable and agreeable both to her and to him."

It was now the turn of the Abbess to pause for awhile in meditation. She remained for a few minutes absorbed in deep thought; and then looking up with a cleared but almost solemn expression of countenance, she said:

"I am utterly at a loss to guess what can be the nature of the facts you have been speaking of. I doubt not that you are exercising a sound discretion in leaving it to your friend to communicate them to me or to withhold them, as he may see fit. But the manner, in which you have spoken of Giulio Malatesta, the warm regard you entertain for him, and the entire confidence he reposes in you, as evidenced by his sending you hither to me, have determined me to confide to you, Giulio's friend, the fact which I have so long and painfully doubted whether I should do well to communicate to himself. When I have done so, you will be better able to judge whether it will be well done to tell the secret to him. And I implore of you, if, when you shall know who and what Giulio Malatesta's mother is, it should seem to you less desirable, than you may now think it, that the fact should be told to him, you will use your discretion as a friend to conceal it from him. The mother of Giulio Malatesta," she went on, speaking with a kind of breathless fevered rapidity, but still in the low tone, which she had used during most of the conversation,—"the mother of Giulio Malatesta is a veiled nun, the inmate of a cloister for more than twenty years;—a deposed and disgraced Abbess; —even she who is now speaking to you!"

"Good God!" exclaimed Carlo, in a voice which made the kneeling and probably sleeping nun at the farther corner of the room start, and stare at him with an angry scowl, before she recomposed herself in her previous position.

"It is even so!" said the Abbess, in a sad voice of deep humility. "Again I ask you, if you still think it right and wise to assist your friend to discover such a mother?"

But Carlo seemed hardly to be listening to what she said. He was pacing up and down before the window, near which they had been sitting, three steps, one way and three the other, biting his thumb-nail with his eyes fixed on the ground.

"I have a good mind!" he muttered—"I have a good mind to tell her! *Per Bacco! che cosa, che cosa!** But it would be unfair to him! It would be cruel to him! No! I will say nothing! *Ecco*, Signora!" he said turning to the Abbess, who sat almost visibly trembling on her chair, as waiting for her doom;—"I beg pardon, I mean to say, your maternity, my opinion is that it is absolutely necessary, and your bounden duty (excuse me for the expression) to tell Giulio what you have told me at the earliest possible opportunity. Depend on

* "What a piece of business!"

me for making that opportunity with as little delay as may be. I will not tell him, for the same reason that I will not tell you now, what he will have to hear from you when he comes;—because I will not take the bloom off the most exquisite pleasure that either of you have ever known! Addio, Signora!—Reverend Mother, I mean! I must hasten back to Florence! Will your maternity tell the old woman to let me out?"

As soon as Carlo found himself, having with much difficulty refrained from swearing at the old portress for her slowness, once more outside the gate, he jumped into his fiacre, roughly waked the sleeping driver, and told him if he wanted double fare to drive like mad to Florence.

"Your illustrious lordship sees that wind blowing off the top of Monte Morello toward the Duomo?" said the man, pointing with his whip as he spoke; "well, we'll catch it, and be in Florence first!"

So saying he leisurely mounted his box, and with a whole salvo of cracks of his whip started off at a gallop of seven miles an hour, which reduced itself to about four within a couple of hundred yards.

CHAPTER IV.

CARLO'S SUPPER.

The magnificent range of palaces and terrace street forming the new Lung' Arno, and extending from the foot of the Ponte alla Carraia to the entrance of the Cascine, did not exist in 1851. Nor was there any such possibility of passing from the handsomest part of the city directly to the well-watered avenues and shady drives of the Cascine, without any intervening morsel of vulgar dusty road, as is now provided for the frequenters of the Florentine Rotten-row by the handsome new gateway which leads directly from the extremity of the Lung' Arno to the confines of the Cascine. Very few fair equestrians frequented the soft rides among the woods, or showed themselves amid the throng of carriages on the *piazzetta* in those days in comparison with the number that may now be seen there. And all the loves of hats and bonnets in the press of carriages inconveniently jostling each other in the narrow gangway of the Porta a Prato had to be exposed to a sprinkling of dust from the Prato road before they reached their exhibition place. And worse still was the inconvenience of the return through that same archway. For all the world left the Cascine at the same time. Every one wanted to go home to dinner. And there would often be a string of carriages extending from the gate half way to the Cascine waiting to get into the city. Then fumed the Englishman, and sat placidly patient the Tuscan; and many a dinner was spoiled by waiting for belated guests.

Nous avons changé tout cela! There is no such scene at the Porta a Prato in these days. But Carlo Brancacci, returning from the convent on the Sesto road, got to the city gate just as the world was returning from the Cascine, and the gate was blocked by a line of carriages for the next half hour! For once, Tuscan as he was, Carlo was impatient. The delay was very vexatious. In vain he stood up in the dusty ramshackle little open carriage, and urged the driver to attempt to cut in to the file of carriages. The dirty little fiacre was obliged to await its turn; and Carlo the while was exposed to a fire of questions and bantering from acquaintances in more aristocratic vehicles.

"What! Brancacci! where in the world do you come from?"

"Oh, Carlo! If I had any little private affair at Campi,* I would not choose just this hour of the twenty-four for coming back!"

"*Birbante!* † Of course he chooses his time on purpose to be seen!"

"What are you in such a hurry about, old fellow?"

"I say, Carlo, you'll have to pay at the gate on all that dust. You can't take in such an unreasonably large quantity free!"

In general, Brancacci would have been quite ready to hold his own, and give back as good as he got in a wordy war of this kind. But upon the present occasion he was too much occupied with graver interests and too impatient, to enter into the spirit of it.

"I say, Nandino," he called out to a young man who was alone in a handsome carriage, "just tell your man to let me pass, there is a good fellow! I am really in a hurry, on business of importance. I will tell you, when I see you."

And the Conte Ferdinando Villamarina, thus appealed to, lazily called out to his coachman to let Signore Brancacci pass, saying to the latter as

* A large village in the direction of Prato, inhabited mainly by straw-plaiters.

† Rogue.

he did so, "not that I believe a word about your business being of any greater importance than your dinner at the avuncular table. It is true, you will need a long time washing! Cut along with you!"

And Carlo having thus by favour avoided losing more than a quarter of an hour, drove directly to the Murate;—to learn there that Giulio Malatesta had left the prison an hour previously, having been liberated by an order from the minister of state.

Getting once more, therefore, into his dust-begrimed shandrydan, Carlo drove to the palazzo in the Via Larga, where he was in time to catch his uncle before he went out to dinner.

"So you have succeeded I find! I have just been to the Murate and found that the bird had flown. It is so good of you to have lost no time! Was there any difficulty about it?"

"Not the least in the world! How should there be? Of course directly I told the minister (a slight emphasis on the *I*) how the matter stood, he said he was sorry for the accident, and sent an order to the prison instantly. I would have gone myself to him at the Murate, but that I was obliged to be at the Cascine!"

"Of course! *Place aux dames!*" said his nephew with a twinkle in his eye.

"But where on earth have you been? Doing

the work of a street-sweeper one would say to look at you."

"Yes! I have collected a curious assortment of specimens of the soil of the Grand-Ducal territory. I have been half-way to Sesto, to a convent, where I have made another discovery—and such a discovery! I never found out anything in my life before, and now two such discoveries in two days! I shall offer myself as head of the secret police department, I think!"

"Ay! That is what you are specially fitted for, no doubt. Pray what is the new mystery?"

"I have found our friend Malatesta's mother; the lady who——you know——"

"You don't mean it! I told you, you remember, that she would be soon found! Well! and who and what was she?"

"I know nothing about who she *was*. She *is* the Abbess of the Convent of Montepulciano, to which the Contessina Stella was sent! And now she has been brought to Florence about some stupid convent quarrel or other. The Archbishop's chaplain told me all about it!"

"The Archbishop's chaplain told you! What, is he one of your friends too? I suppose you and the Archbishop are old cronies?"

"Not exactly! You see, when the Contessina Stella wrote to Giulio that the Superior of her house could very likely give him some information about his mother, it was mainly her doing. Somehow or other it seems the old lady let out the secret to Stella. Most likely the Contessina began by making the Abbess her confidant about her love affair. She is just the woman for a girl to make a confidant in—a charming woman I should say, though she *is* an Abbess! Then the truth slipped out, and by the Superior's own account it was mainly by the Signorina Stella's persuasion that she permitted her to write in that mysterious manner to Giulio."

"Why not tell him the plain fact at once?" asked the Marchese Florimond.

"Well! I think I can understand why," replied Carlo, "but then I have talked to her and you have not. She was afraid—afraid of doing more harm than good in the world by the discovery—afraid, poor soul, that when he knew her position, he might repent having found her—afraid of everything, as a poor nervous woman, first half-killed with trouble, and then shut up in a cloister for twenty years may well be!"

"And how did you get the truth from her?" inquired the Marchese.

"Well! upon my word I hardly know! She saw I was a near friend to Giulio; and then she did not know what to do and caught at any help, as people will when they are between hawk and buzzard;—said that *I* should consider whether it was best to tell him or keep it to myself!"

"But did you tell her your secret?" asked his uncle.

"Not a word! I was on the point of doing so! It was as much as I could do to refrain from letting it all out. But I thought it was not fair to Giulio to do so. I thought he ought to tell her himself. And, besides, it was better for me to stick to my commission. I had, of course, no permission to tell anything."

"Of course not! he could not guess that you were going to see his mother," remarked the Marchese.

"I thought it best, however, to say nothing; and I am glad I refrained, specially as he is now at liberty and may go himself. I mean to do the same with regard to her. I will leave her to tell her secret herself."

"What shall you tell him as the result of your visit, then?"

"That it is perfectly true that the Abbess knows his mother, and can at once bring him and her together—that he has nothing to do but to go to her and receive the information she has to give."

"It will be a queer meeting between them! And when is it to come off?"

"The sooner the better, of course! When I found that he was no longer at the Murate, I hurried here on the chance of catching you before you went out to dinner. And now I must go and look for him. I shall probably find him, or, at all events, hear of him, at the Palmieri's. I shall just have a wash and be off directly! By Jupiter! I never had so much to do before in my life. I shall begin to think I am quite a man of business. It strikes me this sort of thing must be capital training for being a prime minister! I am beginning to feel quite a capable man!"

"What a disagreeable shock such a change must occasion you! And what do you mean to propose to Signor Giulio?"

"That we should go out to the convent where his mother is the first thing to-morrow morning, to be sure! The chaplain gave me an order which renders it unnecessary to ask for a fresh one."

"Were you able to see her alone?"

"No! that would be against all rule, it seems. There was an old woman, one of the nuns, in the room to play propriety; but she stayed at the farther end of it and went to sleep over her beads, so it came to the same thing."

"And now what is to be said, or is anything to be said, to the Canonico Adalberto?"

"Ay! that is the question!" replied Carlo,

thoughtfully. "To-morrow is the first of June. Have you been able to ascertain when the Contessina is to start for her journey?"

"Yes! The Contessa said that she could not start till the morning of the second."

"That is well! It would never do to let her be sent off to that horrid place on the other side of the Apennines. But, as it is, we shall have time enough. I think this will be the best plan. I will take Giulio out to the convent the first thing in the morning. We can be back here by—say midday—or one o'clock at the latest. Suppose you were to see the Canonico in the course of the morning, tell him how the land lies, and make an appointment for an interview between him and Giulio at any hour of the afternoon he likes. I will tell him that we have so arranged, and if he does not approve I will take care that you know it in the morning. But if you hear nothing to the contrary, let it stand that you are to see the Canonico and make an appointment for Giulio to see him to-morrow afternoon. Perhaps it would be as well for you to be present; or, at all events to present him to the Canonico."

"Yes! I think that would be the proper thing to do, since it was as my guest that he first was introduced into the Palazzo Altamari," said the Marchese Florimond, who then adverted to that circumstance for the first time.

"Very well, then. Will you be at home here from twelve till one to-morrow. I will bring Giulio here, and we can go together to the Canonico."

"Very good! let it be so settled. And now what about the Contessa? What is to be said to her?" asked the Marchese, in a tone which seemed to say that that was the most important part of the matter.

"Perhaps it will be best to say nothing till after the interview with the Signor Canonico. Besides, I think I deserve to have my share of the pleasure of telling our news to the Contessa Zenobia!"

To have his share of the *fun*, Carlo would have said if he had been speaking to anybody else but his respected uncle. But it was not safe joking with the Marchese Florimond on that subject. One does not jest about the gout with a martyr to that malady.

"Yes! yes! that is all fair. You know you are a favourite with the Contessa. But I think we ought not to delay telling her longer than to-morrow evening."

"No! I think we might do so to-morrow evening. In fact we must necessarily do so, if the Contessina Stella's journey, which now stands fixed for the next day, is to be set aside. Besides, of course there will be no reason or possibility for further delay when the Signor Canonico shall have been informed of the whole matter."

"Now you are going to look up Giulio? But what will you do about dinner? *Diavolo!* A man must dine, even if he is a prime minister or head of the secret police."

"Oh! I'll get a mouthful at the *bottegone* as I pass!" said Carlo. "You are off I suppose! I shall start in two minutes, as soon as I have got rid of a little of this dust. I won't forget to let you know if Giulio makes any objection to our arrangement. If not, you know, you fix the meeting with the Canonico, and wait for us here from twelve to one to-morrow."

"I understand! *figliuolo mio!*"

"*A rivederci, carissimo Zio.*"

A few minutes afterwards Carlo was once more *en route* towards the house near the Porta Romana, at which he arrived just after Giulio and Rinaldo had gone out together. The former had, as he supposed, betaken himself thither immediately on his liberation from the Murate; and had passed the remaining hours of the afternoon in talking over his recent adventure and the history of his stay at Bologna, and the events subsequently resulting from it, with all the friends assembled there;—old Signora Palmieri, her daughter Teresa, the Professor, and Rinaldo and his wife. There was of course much to be said between him and the Professor. He would willingly also have remained talking for hours with Teresa Palmieri, with whom he then made acquaintance for the first time; because she talked to him of Stella, and he was never weary of listening to all the thousand little remembrances of her convent days, which Teresa fished out of her memory for his benefit. But Rinaldo would not allow him to remain quietly in the house after the little party had dined together. It would have been too contrary to the habits of Italian men to do so. The Professor indeed, ensconcing himself in an arm-chair with a book, contented himself with remaining at home with the ladies as an Englishman might have done. But the other two went out to a café, intending to go thence to a theatre.

Fortunately La Signora Francesca was able to tell Brancacci the name of the café her husband was in the habit of frequenting. It was one in the Mercato Nuovo, known at that time as a resort of liberals;—and one which most of the men, with whom Brancacci habitually lived, would not have liked, whether on account of its political or its non-fashionable character, to be seen in. Brancacci, however, cared little for such considerations; and hurrying off, as directed, found the two friends sitting over their little cups of black coffee at a rickety marble-topped table in one corner of the large comfortless-looking room.

Assuredly the nations of continental Europe are far more gregarious in their tastes and instincts than we are. And a remarkable manifestation of that tendency is seen in the preference an Italian has for sitting in the most uncomfortable place, where others congregate, rather than in the most comfortable home, if peopled only by the members of his family circle. Nor does an Italian ever seem to feel any difficulty in discussing matters of what would appear to us a private nature in such public places. Yet the Italian national character is very far from deficient in caution or secretiveness. And the habitual freedom with which business of all sorts is talked over in crowded cafés can only be accounted for by supposing an equally habitual absorption of every man in his own affairs and his own conversation, to the exclusion of any attention to those of his neighbours.

Giulio Malatesta and Rinaldo Palmieri had their heads very close together, it is true, as they sat in a corner of the café over one of the little tables; and they were talking so intently that they did not observe Brancacci till, coming up to the table at which they were sitting, he cried out:

"At last I've hunted you down! They could not keep you then even at the Murate," he added, dropping his voice, and drawing a little three-legged stool, so as to sit down close to his friends, "till I came back to look for you."

"That is hardly a place you would expect me to

wait for you in, longer than I could help it," returned Giulio laughing. "Thanks to your good kind uncle I got my discharge, as Saint Paul got his! And if I had not been in a great hurry to be free, I should have been tempted to answer as he did. However, here I am, a free man once more!"

"To think of your never telling any of us a word, Signor Carlo, of all the wonderful news our friend Giulio has been giving us!" said Rinaldo.

"No! I thought it fair to leave him to do that for himself. And I have been equally discreet in other quarters. Not a soul knows anything of the matter yet, except my uncle!"

"Thanks! my dear fellow!" said Giulio, stretching out his hand to Brancacci. "I do not know what I should have done, if I had not found so good a friend at need as yourself."

"Such a statesman at need! such an ambassador—such a prime minister at need! I had no conception before, what a capable and invaluable man I am. You don't know half my doings yet. Don't you ask me the result of my perquisitions, my diplomacy, my conferences, my speeches, my reticences, my noddings of the head, and my winkings of the eye? *Per Bacco!* I have my news to tell as well as you!"

"You don't mean that you have found out the

Superior of the convent of Santa Filomena for me?" said Giulio.

"*Altro!* found out, indeed! I knocked up the Archbishop at midnight, and clapping a pistol to his right ear, told him that he had only two minutes and a half to live, if he did not instantly tell me where he had hidden the Abbess of Santa Filomena. The wretched man at first pretended that she was in the dungeons of the Inquisition of Rome. But when I told him, that in that case I would request my friend the Pope to place her immediately at my disposition, and to excommunicate himself, he confessed that she was secreted in a subterranean vault on the top of the Apennines. I instantly compelled him to sign an order for my admission to that fearful prison-house; I rode day and night for sixteen weeks till I got there; I saw the captive; I administered spiritual consolation to her; I heard her wondrous tale!—And now don't you want to know what it was?"

"Are you sure you have not been administering spiritual consolation to yourself out of a flask of Chianti?" said Giulio, laughing.

"Ungrateful! I have not even administered to myself a morsel of dinner this blessed day. Oh, *bottega!** bring me a couple of buttered eggs,

* A Tuscan never calls for the "waiter" in a café; but calls "bottega"—"shop."

bread, and half a flask. And let the eggs be fresh, and the wine not, do you hear! If I have spoken, gentlemen, in any degree inconsistently with the reserved gravity and discreet wisdom which are generally allowed throughout Europe to be my distinguishing characteristics, attribute it, I pray you, to light-headedness caused by inanition."

"But in sober seriousness, my dear fellow, do you really mean that you have seen this Abbess?" said Giulio.

"Nothing can be more sober and more serious than my meaning, except the fact that I really am fainting for a mouthful of food!"

"And you have been, then, racing about all day for me! Well! you shall swallow your mouthful before I ask you to tell your news. I suppose there is little to tell."

"Ah! that's why you are so patient. You would not give me leave to eat a crumb or drink a drop, if you knew what I had to tell!"

"Did you serve an apprenticeship as turncock to Tantalus, by any chance, Signor Carlo?" asked Rinaldo.

"Let him eat his morsel in peace, and then he will enlighten us," said Giulio; "and don't think, my dear fellow," he added to Carlo, "either that I am not anxious for your report, or not very grateful to you for the trouble you have taken to get it.

Only, I have never had any great expectation that this Abbess would be able to give me any very valuable help. If she had known anything definite, she would have spoken more clearly in the first instance. I was determined, however, not to throw the slightest chance away."

"There!" said Carlo, as he used the last fragment of his little loaf—a *semel*, the Tuscans call it—to sop up, sponge-wise, the last particles of the eggs from the little red earthen saucer in which they were served hissing hot from the fire, and popping the morsel into his mouth, washed it down with the last of the half-flask of Chianti; "there! now I once again feel myself a match for Talleyrand! I was below the mark when starving. Signor Giulio Malatesta, I purpose that your lady mother shall stand by the altar at your marriage with the Contessina Stella Altamari!"

The two other young men looked at each other, and Malatesta said gravely, "Come now, Carlo! be in earnest for once in your life, there is a dear good fellow! Remember, this is no laughing matter to me!"

"Nor to me, my dear old friend, believe me!" returned Carlo, in a more serious tone. "But I mean what I say. If your mother does not stand by at your wedding before the first flask of this year's wine is made in Tuscany—call me a *sbirro!*"

"You really have some certain information, then, Carlo *mio?*" said Giulio, with a bright gleam in his eye.

"*Altro!* Listen! Briefly and soberly the matter stands thus. The Abbess of Santa Filomena is now in a convent some three miles out towards Sesto. There, by means of an order from the Archbishop, I have this day seen her. I had the honour of a long conversation with her. She not only knows with certainty where your mother now is, but is able to bring you at once to speech with her. The order I have will suffice to obtain you an interview with the Abbess; and I purpose accompanying you to the convent where she is the first thing to-morrow morning. I may add, my dear fellow, that I have very good reason to believe that the mother you will find is one in all respects with whom you will be delighted, and of whom you may be proud! There! is that plain, methodical, and prosaic enough?"

"My dear fellow! how can I ever thank you enough!" cried Giulio.

"Well then, that is settled. You will go out with me to-morrow morning? We had better start soon after eight."

"Will I not? I will be at your door in the Via Larga by eight."

"And bring a *fiacre* with you! I did not say a word to the Abbess about your other news."

"No! of course not! why should you? It can be nothing to her, you know," said Giulio.

"Well! I felt tempted to do so all the same," said Carlo; "but I refrained. Perhaps you will feel tempted to tell it her in return for her information, when you see her. We shall see. I have taken it upon me to make another engagement for you, after our return from the convent; and if you do not approve of it, I must tell my uncle to-night. It is to call on his reverence the Canonico Altamari. My uncle proposes to present you to him."

"It is very kind of him; and as it has to be done, it is perhaps as well to do it at once."

"*Diamine!* Recollect that there will be no seeing somebody else till you have seen him, and had it all out."

"True!" said Giulio, thoughtfully.

"And we look to your interview with the Canon to-morrow afternoon, to prevent the starting of that somebody else to Heaven knows where the next day!"

"God grant that it *may* prevent it!" said Giulio, with a great sigh.

"Never fear! *I* know how the land lies! Have *I* not told you that you shall be married before the new wine is made? Where do you sleep to-night?"

"At the inn behind the *palazzo* here, where I went on my arrival. The good people could not imagine what had become of me!"

"Now! shall we go to the Pergola?" said Rinaldo.

"No! let us go to the Teatro Nuovo," answered Carlo. "If we go to the Pergola, I shall have to go to half a dozen boxes, and be asked all sorts of questions. Come along! What are they giving at the Teatro Nuovo?"

It did not make much difference to the young men what the performance was; and most people except Italians would have thought it more convenient to talk over all they had to say to each other anywhere else than standing with their hats on among a crowd of other loiterers at the back of the pit of the theatre. But they *were* Italians, and acted accordingly.

CHAPTER V.

MOTHER AND SON.

PUNCTUALLY at eight o'clock the next morning Giulio was at the door of the Palazzo Brancacci, in the Via Larga, with a hack-carriage. And in a very few minutes Carlo joined him, and they started on their drive towards Sesto.

"Yes! there she is!" said the latter, in answer to Giulio's wistful look at the Palazzo Altamari, as they passed before it; "there are only some fifty *braccia** of space and one of stone wall between you! I wonder whether she has any idea of your being in Florence!"

"How should she have? You forget how long it is since it has been possible for me to write to her!" answered Giulio, with a heavy sigh.

* The Tuscan measure, the *braccia*, is a little less than two feet.

"No! I know that! But of course the Contessa Zenobia must have heard of your arrival, and she may have let fall a word in the Contessina's hearing."

"Not she! they would never let her know that I was near her—dear, brave, constant Stella!"

"Well, well! we shall see before the sun sets whether they are inclined to let her know that you are in Florence! What a surprise for her it will be! She is thinking now of her dismal to-morrow's journey to Palazzuolo!"

"Which, thanks to you, we may hope to be in time to prevent! You have got the Archbishop's order with you?"

"All right, old fellow! What do you take me for? It says nothing about admitting two; but we shall not find any difficulty, I dare say."

And then the conversation dropped, and they drove on in the deliciously balmy morning air in silence, till Carlo cried out:

"Oh! Giulio! Are you asleep. We are about as merry as if we were going to a funeral."

"I am but a bad companion for such a jolly dog as you, Carlo *mio*, at the best of times," returned Malatesta, "and am worse than ever this morning. But you must make allowance for all that I have pressing on my mind just at present. Think what it is to be about to see a mother, of whom you know absolutely nothing, for the first time!"

"Yes, I admit it is a nervous sort of thing," replied Carlo; "but I am convinced, from what the Abbess said, that your discovery will not be a disagreeable one. She is herself a most pleasing person—a gentle, charming, lady-like manner!—and very handsome!"

"It matters very little to me what she is!" rejoined Giulio. "I am thinking of what the other will be like."

"Very true!" said Carlo, looking into his friend's eyes with a look of queer meaning and longing to tell him—"very true! but she is a sort of person who would not imagine another woman to be all those things if she were not so."

"And did she say all that of my poor mother?" asked Giulio.

"She spoke in a manner," replied Carlo, rather puzzled and hesitatingly, "which led me to infer that she must so think of her. But it is no use speculating on the subject!" he added, fearing to be driven into further perplexities, and quite determined not to betray his secret. "What is the good of guessing, when we shall so soon see for ourselves!"

"That is true!" sighed Giulio. "Are we near the place?"

"You see that group of cypresses, a little above the level of the road, on the side of the hill yonder, with a little squat belfry and a lot of white buildings close behind them? That is the convent. We have to climb a little bit of steep hill out of the road. I can hear the little bell tinkling away for matins, or nones, or angelus, or something, or else for the mere fun of the thing!"

"Yes! I can hear it! I hope the nuns won't be at any service which will prevent us from seeing the Abbess."

"Oh! never fear! If they are in the choir, she will come out to the Archbishop's order!"

It was about nine o'clock when they reached the convent. The church doors were open, as before. The same two old women were on the little sunny terrace, and manifested the same, or even an increased, astonishment at the repetition of the wonderful phenomenon of a city carriage arriving at the convent;—and this time with *two signori* in it! Would it come to-morrow with three? Were the nuns, now in these bad latter days, going to fall into a course of mundane dissipation? *Santa Madonna!* There were no such doings in their young days! But, then, neither in those days had they the rheumatisms and the cramps of these latter times! And bread had been only nine quattrini a pound! Evidently the times were out of joint, and the world was going to the bad! Considerations which did not prevent them from endeavouring, like wise old women, to extract from the evil of the times any possible good that could be got out of it, by hobbling up to the carriage with outstretched withered hands, and urgent demands in the name of the Madonna and Saint Eusebius.

And then the same process preparatory to obtaining access to the interior of the monastery had to be gone through, and the same delays to be borne with such patience as the young men could muster.

"I think," said Carlo, while they were waiting in the bare-looking whitewashed "*parlatorio*," which seemed colder and barer in the morning, for the sun-rays were not streaming into it—"I think I had better vanish when I have introduced you to the Abbess."

"Oh, no! Why should you do that? There is nothing to be said that you don't know. You had better stay," said Giulio.

"No! There is nothing to be said that I don't know!" replied Carlo. "Nevertheless, I think I will leave you two together;—that is, if I can manage to get out! If not, I shall get up a separate flirtation with the old chaperone. Here they come!"

And again the Abbess, attended by the same old

woman as on the occasion of Carlo's previous visit, entered as before. The "chaperone," as Carlo profanely called her, took her chair as before, placed it immediately beside the door, as if her function had been to prevent any attempt at escape on the part of the Abbess or her visitors, and immediately absorbed herself—doubtless according to orders—in the exercise of the rosary.

The Abbess walked, also, as before, across the wide brick floor to the opposite window—as before! but an observant eye might have marked a difference in her bearing. Her step was slow, and her movements struck both the young men as remarkably dignified and elegant. But her eyes were bent on the ground, veiled beneath their long soft lashes, which showed their silken fringe in strong contrast with the perfect paleness of her face. A more boldly curious glance than that of either of her young visitors might also have perceived that the folds of her religious dress were rising and falling over her bosom in a manner indicating unmistakably that the heart beneath that coarse serge drapery in no wise shared the tranquillity of her outward bearing. The eyes remained downcast during the whole of her passage across the room. But who can doubt that they had already taken in at a glance every detail and minute particular of the appearance of the newcomer with that unfailing rapidity of accurate observation which is so frequently a speciality of the finest female organisations.

When she had reached the spot near the window at which the conversation with Brancacci had taken place, and before she had taken a seat, Carlo advanced towards her, and, with a low bow, which she returned by the usual benedictory movement of the fingers, but so faintly made as to suggest the idea that she was suffering from physical exhaustion, said:

"Reverend mother, this is Giulio Malatesta, whom I have brought to you in fulfilment of my promise that I would make the interval before he waited on you as short as possible. Let it please your maternity to note that I have not taken it on myself to inform him of the facts mentioned by you to me yesterday, thinking it better to leave that duty to your maternity; as I also thought it best that he should himself communicate to you, if he shall see fit to do so, the circumstances which have recently produced a change in his own position."

Malatesta bowed reverently as he stood before the tall, straight, and slender figure of the Abbess, erect before him, but with her eyes still fixed on the ground; while Carlo, after the above introductory speech, spoken in a tone of solemn seriousness that was very unusual in him, lounged across the room to the place where the old nun was kneeling over her beads, and standing before her as a man stands in front of a lady in a drawing-room, remarked, in an easy offhand manner:

"A charming position you have here for your convent, Signora!"

The old woman reared herself and glared at him with a mixture of terror, indignation, and astonishment, which seemed to deprive her for some seconds of the power of speech.

"The view over the valley from the terrace in front of your church is really exquisite!" he continued, utterly unconscious of her dismay.

"Your business here is with her!" said the old woman at length, with harsh sternness, pointing her fore-finger as she spoke to the Abbess.

"My part of the business is done. It is that gentleman who has now to speak with the Abbess; I may, therefore, have the pleasure of a little conversation with you!" returned Carlo, with undiminished good humour.

"I have no permission to speak with you!" rejoined the nun, leaving Carlo to infer, if it should so please him, the compliment that she would be very glad to avail herself of it if she had; but still speaking in the same gruff voice.

"In that case," said Carlo, "I think I had better go out."

The old woman looked perplexedly backwards

and forwards from him to the two persons at the other end of the room, once or twice, and then said, again pointing with her forefinger:

"I may not leave him here alone!"

"Then, I suppose, I must try to find the way to the outer door by myself!" rejoined Carlo, taking the handle of the room-door in his hand.

"No! Stay, I beg you, Signore! That cannot be! You cannot pass through the convent alone. It is not permitted!" exclaimed the old woman, becoming less laconic, in the extremity of her alarm and perplexity.

"*Per Bacco! questa è buffa!*"* exclaimed Carlo, tickled by the absurdity of the position into a laxity of expression unbecoming the atmosphere of a nunnery. "Is there no way, then, by which I can get out? I shall burst, if I am obliged to stay here and hold my tongue!"

Urged by the danger of this alternative, and dismayed by the verbosity of the conversation into which she was being betrayed, the old woman at last said, pointing again as before:

"He must come, too—to the door!—Then he may come back again!"

"That is a bright thought!" said Carlo. "I should never have thought of that. Giulio," he cried, "you must please to come and escort me out

* "This is droll."

of this wonderful place. For, it seems, the old lady here must not lose sight of either of us!"

So Giulio, accompanied his friend and the old nun, tinkling her warning bell as she went, to the convent door.

"I will wait here for you on the terrace, old fellow, till you come out. Do not be in any hurry! An hour under the cypresses with a cigar, will be pleasant enough!"

And Giulio, reconducted in the same manner, returned to the "*parlatorio;*" and the nun immediately resumed her position and her occupation close to the door.

The Abbess was sitting by the window with her face turned towards it, and leaning on her hand, apparently in deep thought.

"The Signorina Altamari was right, then, reverend mother, when she wrote to me that it was in your power to give me information respecting my poor mother. For, I understand from my excellent friend, Signor Carlo Brancacci, that you have certain knowledge of her present whereabouts."

The Abbess did not answer for a few seconds, and then, at first, replied only by a bow, till she, not without difficulty apparently, said, "It is true, Signore! I have that knowledge." There was some feeling at her heart which prevented her from using the ecclesiastical formula "my son," in addressing him.

"May I hope, then, that your maternity will lend your aid to the accomplishment of an object of which you cannot but approve?" said Malatesta, with cold courtesy.

"Did your friend mention to you," asked the Abbess, speaking in a slow, *staccato* manner, as though her throat were dry, and the words came from it with difficulty—"Did your friend mention to you the reasons that had suggested themselves to me for doubting whether I could approve the object you allude to?"

"No, indeed! reverend mother; I am at a loss to conceive what reasons can possibly have so suggested themselves to you," replied Giulio, with surprise.

"The relationship between a mother and son," continued the Abbess, speaking with the same difficulty, and, as it were, reluctance as before, "like that of husband and wife, may be a source of infinite blessing and happiness to both—or it may be the reverse. Does your experience of the world, short as it may be, my son" (she dropped the two last words so tremulously, and, as it were, breathlessly, that they were barely audible); "does your experience of the world furnish your memory with no examples of the latter misery? Have you seen no cases in which it were better for a son never to have known a mother;—in which he has had to blush for a mother, who, in bearing him, inflicted the mark of an indelible disgrace;—in which all those holy and exquisite affections that should make the happiness of such a tie, have been turned to gall and bitterness;—in which," she continued, raising her voice to a tone in which a practised ear might have detected the accent of sharp anguish, "the one only proof of a mother's love that a mother could give, would have been, if happily she were unknown, to heedfully remain so;—if unhappily still living, to be at least dead to him!"

Giulio had become very pale while the Abbess was speaking. He clasped his hands tightly together as he stood rigidly in front of her, looking at her with his great dark eyes as if he would read the secret she seemed so reluctantly to part with in her heart, and the drops of perspiration gathered on his brow.

"Reverend mother," he said, speaking slowly but firmly, "your words seem intended to prepare me for a heavy blow. They can hardly be meant to save me from it. You can scarcely deem me guilty of the cowardice of shrinking from sacred duties, even if they must bring only pain and not pleasure with them, by voluntarily remaining in ignorance of what I have come here to learn."

"Nay, my son! The volition in the matter is still with me. Should I deem it better, wiser, more for your welfare and happiness, not to make this discovery to you, it will be my—my bounden duty to remain silent."

"I cannot think," returned Giulio, keeping his position, standing immediately in front of her, and looking down on her with earnest eyes while he spoke with extreme gravity; "I cannot think that your maternity would, under any circumstances, feel yourself justified in adopting such a course. I trust you will pardon me for using language hardly becoming from me to one in your position, and let my paramount interest in this question be my excuse. I cannot, I repeat, conceive that on mature reflection you will find it consistent with your duty to keep from me the knowledge which you have admitted you possess, respecting my unhappy and foully-wronged mother. The manner in which you have spoken prepares me, as I must suppose it was intended to do, for the shock and great pain of finding in my unhappy mother—not such an one as a son would wish to find. But let her position, qualities, and conduct, be what they may, my determination, nay, my ardent desire in the matter, would remain the same. Think, reverend mother—or rather it is for me to think—of all the wrongs, the woes, the injustice, the sufferings, which that poor mother has had to struggle with. If her unhappy position, and the cruel wrong which was done her,—worse wrong than your maternity can guess!—have caused her to fall farther, and ever farther from the standard of duty and rectitude, and a blameless life, so much the more is it my duty, as it is my dearest wish, to repair as far as may be the injustice which has been done her; to pour balm into the heart-wounds that have exposed her to dangers to which happier women are strangers; to open to her a haven of refuge and protection which she has never known; and to soothe her heart with a love of which she has been defrauded."

The measured and grave tone in which Giulio had begun to speak had gradually been changed, as his heart swelled with the emotions which his words produced; and he now hurried on, pouring out the phrases with all that eloquence of accent and intonation with which the excitable southern nature, when warmed by strong feeling, so readily expresses itself:

"You know not, reverend mother, *you* cannot know, how my heart yearns to this poor lonely-hearted mother, defrauded of all her share of love! how I long to tell her that the child of her bosom, the child of her sorrow and shame, has come to her, to comfort, to atone, and to love her, and to wipe out sorrow and shame! Give me my mother! I demand her of you! You have no right to keep her from me!"

"My son! my son!" sobbed rather than said the Abbess, and the words forcing themselves convulsively from her bosom, seemed laden with the weight of all the contending emotions which were tearing it. She held out her two open hands a little in front of her—only a little, as if not daring to claim the embrace, which she was so tremblingly longing to receive.

But Giulio, too much absorbed by the strength of his own emotion to mark the manifestations of hers, conceived her words to be but the mode of address proper to her ecclesiastical rank.

"If I have spoken too boldly," he said, remember that it is the heart of a son pleading for the mother that bore him!"

"My son! my son!" reiterated the now violently sobbing woman, looking up with streaming eyes into his face, and extending her hands a little, but still timidly and hesitatingly, towards him.

"What!" cried Giulio, bending forwards, and staring with dilated eyes, still doubtful whether he at last understood her aright. "What?"

But the poor mother had no further eloquence at command. Looking up at him, as he stood transfixed with the greatness of his astonishment, and hardly yet realising the truth of what he had heard, she lifted her eyes with a piteous pleading in them to his face, and pointing with the fingers of one hand to her bosom, nodded with her head, as she sobbed out the one word, "Giulio!"

Then the whole truth burst in all its fulness upon him.

For an instant he stood almost stunned by the violence of all the varied emotions which rushed tumultuously over his heart. Then throwing himself on his knees before her, as she sat, he flung his arms around her, while she clasped his head to her heart, and let her cheek fall upon his brow.

The nun at the farther end of the room must have happily fallen into as fast a slumber over her beads, as the occupation of "telling" them was calculated to produce; for she stirred not, and "made no sign" of cross or other, as she most assuredly would have done in some sort, had she been aware of the scene that was being enacted in her presence.

It was some little time before either the mother or the son could speak connected words; nor did Giulio move, till he felt the warm tears from his mother's eyes trickling silently on his forehead. Then drawing back his head, and taking her two hands in his, but without rising from his knees, he said:

"Oh mother! mother! that sweet word! mother, how could you—how *could* you hesitate and hold back the precious secret you had to tell me!"

"Have I done right, then, my Giulio! my own boy!. How can I forgive myself for—for—for presenting to you a nun, an unwedded nun, as your mother, my poor injured boy!"

"Mother! mother! Do not speak in that way! It is all a delusion,—a mistake,—a cheat!—and were it otherwise——"

"It was she,—she whom you love, my Giulio, and who loves you with, oh! what a love! what a noble all-trusting love!—it was she, Giulio, who first insisted that your unfortunate mother should be made known to you! It was her wish, Giulio!"

"Dear generous-hearted noble darling!" cried Giulio, as the tears,—proud, sweet tears! gathered in his eyes; "of course she insisted! Did she not give me her love, knowing—as I was when she first saw me! Ah! mother! when you know Stella as I know her! What a blessed chance it was that brought you together!"

"A blessing I shall never cease to be thankful for! If only—if——"

There was something very touching in the tremulous sensitive shrinking of the poor mother from the dread that her position might be felt as a social injury to her son;—a dread that scarcely dared to permit itself to be reassured, lest he might feel that it had been better for him to have remained in ignorance of his mother, than to have found such an one!—a dread above all lest it should injure him in the matter of his love!

"She knew all, Giulio!" she continued, eagerly pleading, "all, all my unhappy history! And—and—and it did not lessen her devotion to you, or her desire, that you should find your mother—such as she is!"

"Such as she is!" exclaimed he, drawing back his head, and throwing it up proudly, while he looked at her with infinite tenderness in his eyes;—"such as she is! Oh! mother, how can you speak in such a manner! What son would not be proud of such a mother?"

For an instant there was a gleam of gratified affection in her eyes, as he spoke; but in the next moment she dropped the long lashes over them, and bent her head, as she said:

"Alas! there is no cancelling the disgrace with which the world marks such motherhood as mine, my son;—no remedy for the injury which such a mother inflicts upon her child!"

"But it is all an error, and a cheat, I tell you, mother dear; and the cheat has been found out at last!" he cried, still kneeling at her knee, and holding her hands in his. "What a dolt I am not to have already made you understand, and set that dear long-aching heart at rest. Have I not told you—did not Brancacci tell you—that all that was changed?"

"Your friend, he that was here just now,—he loves you well, too, my Giulio! they all love you! —told me that changes in your position made it more desirable than ever for you to discover your mother. But he said nothing,—he refused to say anything to explain his meaning."

"He thought, good kind-hearted fellow as he is, that he would leave to me the pleasure of telling you my tidings. But he did not guess, I'll be bound, that I should be so maladroit as to keep them so long untold. This, it is then, my own mother, in a word. You are the lawfully-wedded wife—the only wife of the Marchese Cesare Malatesta, my father; and I am his only lawful son and heir!"

"Ah no! Giulio, Giulio, there is some terrible mistake! Here is the first office I have to perform for you, my poor boy! It is I who have to trample out the last spark of your hope! Disappointment is the first thing I bring with me. Do not delude yourself, my poor Giulio! The marriage which I made clandestinely with your father in Bologna was pronounced by the tribunals there to be informal and of no effect. I had friends there, my son, who would have taken care that it should have been shown to be otherwise had there been any possibility of doing so!"

"My own darling mother! It is as I tell you! There is no mistake! I know all about it; and if you will hear me patiently I will soon show you how all the errors fell out. You do not bring me disappointment. On the contrary, it is I who bring you an unhoped-for deliverance from much sorrow! Listen to me now, my own mother. Do you know why the marriage at Bologna between you and my father was pronounced invalid?"

"Assuredly I know, Giulio *mio! pur troppo!* * The law requires that a marriage so made should be witnessed by two persons of legal age. One of the witnesses of my marriage was not of legal age. The marriage, therefore, was not made according to the requisite conditions, and was pronounced accordingly to be null and void!"

"Exactly so! The witness, who turned out to be no witness, because he was under age, was——"

"Pietro Varani; the son of my poor mother's nearest neighbour."

"Precisely so! Pietro Varani, now Professor of Materia Medica in the University of Pisa, and my very good and valued friend."

* "But too well!"

"No! you don't say so! Poor Pietro! Ah me! How the past days come back to me! Yes! poor Pietro was a contemporary and fellow-student of my husb——Alas! my Giulio, of him whom I believed to be my husband, besides being our friend and nearest neighbour—and, as such, was chosen one of the witnesses. Unhappily he was not of legal age."

"Pietro Varani in the September of the year 1828 *was* of legal age."

"Nay, Giulio *mio*; my son, my son, I fear me you are leaning on a reed. Poor Pietro knew perfectly well that he was under age! but was not aware that the law required such a condition. If any doubt could have existed it was set at rest by the entry of his matriculation in the University books, and, I believe, even by his baptismal certificate."

"Yes! also, mother dear, as you say, by his baptismal certificate. But that certificate, on which the other statements of his age were based, had been fraudulently altered, showing him to be one year younger than he really was!"

"Gracious Heaven! by whom and for what purpose? Not by my husband?" almost shrieked the Abbess.

"No! assuredly not by my father! Remember that the fraud had been perpetrated previously to Pietro Varani's admission to the University, inasmuch as the erroneous statement was repeated in the matriculation books."

"By whom then?" asked the Abbess, lost in astonishment.

"By Marta Varani, the mother of Pietro," answered Giulio, nodding his head gravely, and looking solemnly into his mother's face.

"And why was this cruel, this wicked wrong done? What could have been that strange old woman's motive?"

"Her motive, my mother, was to save *her* son from that stigma which it was so bitter a sorrow to you to believe that you had inflicted on *your* son. Pietro Varani was born in the south of France, before his mother was married to his father. When they were about to return to Bologna, where she was well known and held in good repute, and where her son would have to take his civil status, and make his career, Marta Varani determined to represent his birth to have occurred one year later than it really did, and altered the French certificate of his birth accordingly."

"Merciful Heaven! And for this I was condemned——"

"Even so, my mother! You were condemned, and your son was condemned to suffer all *that* unjustly, which Marta Varani and her son ought to have suffered justly."

"I can see now the cruel, hard old woman as she looked——"

"Nevertheless, my mother, let us understand rightly the extent of the crime committed against you—against us—by that cruel and hard old woman—for it cannot be denied that such she was. Of course you perceive that the fraud originally perpetrated by her was intended to benefit herself and her son, without any injury to others. I do not doubt that if it had been in her power to prevent the fatality which led to the choice of Pietro Varani as a witness to a marriage which was fatally invalidated by the falsehood regarding his age, she would have done so. Her fault lay in this—that when the mischief had been done, she held her peace and spoke no word to prevent the fatal consequences from following. She could not bring herself to save you at the cost of exposing her own fraud and forfeiting the advantages which she had gained by a twenty years' persistence in it."

"It was very wicked and very cruel!" said the Abbess with a deep sigh.

"It *was* very wicked and very cruel," resumed her son; "but in this also we must be just, my mother, in the apportionment of blame—painful as it is to be so, we must remember that but for the much worse treachery of——another, the invalidity of the marriage before the Archbishop of

Bologna, would have been a matter of comparatively small moment. All that was needed when the nullity of that ceremony was discovered, was to repeat it in a proper and binding manner. Marta Varani was, in the first instance—that is to say, as soon as the nullity of the marriage was declared—justified in saying to herself that forthwith to confess her fraud in the matter of the certificate of her son's birth, would have been to injure herself very seriously for no other purpose than to save you from a small inconvenience. She was justified in presuming that the error in the matter would have been at once satisfactorily rectified, as it easily might have been. Then, when the fatal news of——the Marchese Malatesta's marriage with the Contessa Cecilia Sampieri came to Bologna, right, justice, every noble sentiment demanded that the truth should be declared. But it had then become more difficult and more painful to do so; and Marta Varani had neither sufficient love of right, nor sufficient care for you to brave the troubles that lay in the way of acting conscientiously. She quieted her conscience, moreover, with the consideration that it was too late to prevent misery and distress in one quarter or another. If your marriage were made good, what became of that of the noble lady the Contessa Cecilia Sampieri?"

"And what *does* become of that marriage?" asked the Abbess, looking up in sudden alarm.

"Assuredly the nullity of that marriage follows from the establishment of yours. Truly the train of evils growing out of that first fraud in the matter of Pietro Varani's real age is a long one. But you see now, my mother, the real amount of old Marta Varani's cruelty and wickedness. It was bad, but infinitely less so than that of——another. Moreover, the old woman's repentance was, as we must suppose, sincere. She did what she could to remedy the injustice which had been done on her death-bed; for she is dead. She died a few months since—placing in my hands, before her death, the means of establishing her son's real age, and, consequently, the validity of your marriage. I need hardly tell you, mother dear, that from first to last in this sad story Pietro Varani—Professor Varani as I ought to call him—has not only been wholly blameless, but has felt and acted as a true-hearted honourable man, and a sincerely-attached friend."

"Poor Pietro Varani! Yes! he was that!" said the Abbess, with a sigh as from some feeling, or some far away memory of some feeling, a slight blush overspread her pale and delicate cheek.

"I think," pursued Giulio, in a graver and sadder tone, "that I ought not to conceal from you, my mother, that it was the firm persuasion of the old woman, Marta Varani, that the Marchese Cesare Malatesta purposely selected her son as a witness to the pretended marriage, with the planned and premeditated intention that it should be declared invalid. God knows if it was so!"

"Oh! no, no! not that!" cried the Abbess, looking up at Giulio, with a face as pale as death, and trembling as if she had received a new and unexpected wound. "Not that!—He yielded to temptation and coercion afterwards; but——not *that*—not *that!* He did love once——No! I cannot believe that. Do not compel me to believe that!"

Curious to mark how even yet the woman's heart clung, after all that had come and gone, to the notion that once—some quarter of a century ago!—she had been truly loved!

"God knows the truth!" returned her son, solemnly. "I have no reason whatever for thinking the old woman's suspicion a just one! Possibly the desire to make or to feel her share in the mischief which had been done as light as possible, biased her towards an unfairly evil opinion of him, on whom fell all that portion of the blame that did not fall on her."

"Yes! Yes! she judged him with cruel injustice in that respect!" returned the woman who had loved him so well; "but about that second marriage, Giulio *mio?* I feel stunned by the suddenness of all you have told me, and my head seems whirling round. What will happen about that marriage—and the unhappy woman—mother too, she also!"

"What will happen—has happened rather—there can be no doubt. That marriage at Fermo was no marriage. The Contessa Cecilia Sampieri was no wife—*was* not, for, happily for her, she has been dead for many years—and the son she has left, and who is now held to be the Marchese Alfonso Malatesta, has no right to that title."

"It is very dreadful!" said the Abbess, placing her hand, as she spoke, over her eyes.

"It *is* very dreadful!" returned her son; "but it would have been much more so, that you, my mother, should have continued to suffer unmerited obloquy and injustice!"

"It is very, very sweet—you cannot guess *how* sweet, my Giulio, to have become suddenly rich in a son, and a son's love! And it is, oh! so sweet! to know that his inheritance from his mother is not one of shame and disgrace. But for the rest—what change can be any change for me!"

"Respecting all that, my own mother, there will be much to be said. We must talk together at much greater length than we can do now

There is that poor dear, best of good fellows, Carlo, waiting outside for me!"

"You don't know how he spoke of you to me yesterday, my Giulio! with what delicacy and true good feeling he did his mission, and what comfort he gave me!"

"And you don't know how good and kind a friend he has been to me, when—when I was not the Marchese Giulio Malatesta!" said Giulio, putting those words together for the first time.

"God bless him!" ejaculated the Abbess, fervently.

"And there is another subject, dearest mother, to be talked over between us," said Giulio, blushing.

"Do you think it has been absent from my mind, Giulio *mio!* But you forget that there is less to be said on that subject than might have been. Though I doubt not that you would find it a very pleasant chapter to discuss till the Ave Maria rings! But remember, that my daughter-in-law will be an older acquaintance of mine than my son!"

"Mother! you speak as if all were settled, and the prize won! You don't know the people on whom she is dependent!"

"But I do know her! *e basta!** If ever a man was blessed with the devoted love of a true, brave,

* "And that is sufficient."

all-trusting, all-daring, unshakably constant heart, you are so blessed, my son!"

"God bless you, my own mother!" said Giulio, as, with his eyes full of tears, he stooped his head, and pressed his lips to his mother's forehead.

"It has been arranged that I am to have an interview with her uncle and guardian, the Canonico Adalberto Altamari, this afternoon. I am to be at the Palazzo Brancacci, in the Via Larga, by one o'clock; and it is time for me to be going. Of course I shall see you to-morrow!"

"Go! and all good fortune attend you, my Giulio! It is hard to part with you! As for my future——"

"That, too, is another large chapter. But the Marchesa Malatesta, *madre mia*, will assuredly find that things will arrange themselves as she may most wish!"

"Ah me! that will indeed open a new chapter in the life of the Marchesa Malatesta!" said the Abbess, with a sigh! "But while the world is bright before you, my son, it cannot be very dark to me!"

"Adieu, till to-morrow, mother dear!"

The Abbess rose from her chair as he spoke, and held out her arms towards him; and the mother and son were in the next instant locked in a long and close embrace.

When they separated, and Giulio turned to leave the *parlatorio*, the old nun, who had somewhat prematurely waked from her slumbers, was standing in the middle of the room with open mouth and uplifted hands, speechless with horror at the spectacle that met her eyes! Giulio burst into a loud laugh, as he said, "Pardon, holy sister! we thought you were asleep!"

It became but too clear to the old woman, that men in the world really were the hardened profligates she had heard; worse, even, than she could have supposed! But she had no words to speak her feelings; and preceded him to the door of the convent, ringing her bell with a fury that spoke her sense of the doubly dangerous nature of the intruder, against whom she was called on to warn the lambs of the sheepfold.

CHAPTER VI.

GIULIO'S DIAGRAM.

Coming round the corner of the front of the little church, from the convent door, Giulio saw his friend luxuriously reclining on the low terrace wall in the cypress shade, engaged in watching with apparently extreme interest the smoke from his cigar, as it curled up to lose itself among the branches.

"Have I kept you too long?" he said.

"Kept me too long!" cried Carlo; "could anybody be kept too long in the beatified state in which I have been revelling! Feel this air! look at this view! taste this cigar! listen to the hum of the insects in the silence! smell the breeze from the convent garden there! How delicious is a country life—till dinner-time!"

"Are we in good time?"

"Plenty of time! We shall be in Florence soon after mid-day. But what have you to tell me? Have you no report to present?"

"*Birbante!* to think of your knowing all, and leading me here blindfold!"

"I acted with a lofty and rigorous impartiality that would have done credit to Olympian Jupiter, arranging the affairs of mortals. I kept your secret from her, and her secret from you! Was that discretion? Was that diplomacy? Talk of Machiavelli, and Richelieu, and the like! Why, they are bunglers, rustics to me! Then as for the prophetic branch of the business—what do you say now to my announcement that your lady mother should assist at your wedding before the new wine is made?"

"The grapes are swelling fast, Carlo! I have found my mother, it is true, thanks to you!—and such a mother!—but you forget how much more still lies between this and the consummation you promise."

"*Ciarle!** It will all go upon wheels, I tell you. The old Canon and that matchless absurdity, La Zenobia, want to marry the Altamari heiress to the Malatesta heir, don't they? Ah, but there is the lady herself! Whom does *she* want to marry? Who knows but what, directly her guardians declare

* "Idle talk"—nonsense!

in your favour, she will fall desperately in love with the Signor Alfonso! Girls *are* so capricious! *That* is what we have to fear! You see it in that light, don't you, Signor Marchese?"

"If I had not been separated from you for the last three years, I should know how to roast you! Were you ever in love?"

"Yes! I've known what 'tis to pine!"

"You look like it—very!"

"Don't wake sleeping memories!—or dogs! Let 'em lie! As soon as the weighing-chair announced that the ravages of passion had reduced me below twelve stone, I made a tremendous effort, a supreme struggle with my heart, and was rewarded by rapidly winning back my thirteen stone! Such are the fruits of virtue!"

"But I say, Carlo *mio!* you were speaking just now of that unfortunate Alfonso, my half-brother! What is to become of him?"

"Become of him! How should I know? He'll go out; and leave an unpleasant smell behind him, like a bad lamp, I should think! Half-brother! He can't be a tenth part your brother! You have no idea what an animal it is!"

"I have heard something of him," said Giulio, with a passing smile, as he remembered certain passages in some of Stella's letters; "but, all the same, his position is a very shocking one!"

"He did not give himself any trouble about *your* position!"

"But then, you say, he is but a sorry sort of an animal. Besides, I was brought up to nothing else. His case is different. And he fancies that he is going to marry Stella, too! Poor wretch! what a fall!"

"*That* fall will break no bones, or hearts either! Bless your soul! The little creature shook in his shoes before La Zenobia, and was mortally afraid of La Contessina herself. Nothing would have kept him from running away from his matrimonial campaign, but his still more mortal terror of the Canonico,—who is, it must be owned, rather a terrible man to play tricks with."

"Any way, he cannot be left to starve! Some position must be found for him!" rejoined Giulio.

"Starve! no! It can't take much to keep such a body and soul as that together—if he has any soul! *Che! che! che!* all that will arrange itself easily enough! You will hardly live at Fermo, when the old Marchese goes off! Let the Signore Alfonso take care of the old place there!"

Thus chatting, the young men reached the door of the Palazzo Brancacci, between twelve and one o'clock, and found the Marchese Florimond waiting for them according to agreement.

"Have you seen the Canonico, uncle?" asked

Carlo, as soon as the latter had with marked cordiality greeted and welcomed Malatesta, and had received the thanks of Giulio for the exertions the Marchese Brancacci had made in his behalf. "Have you prepared the way for the projected interview?"

"I have had a long, and I may be permitted to say, an important interview with the Canonico Altamari. The Canonico will be prepared to receive my friend the Marchese Malatesta at any hour he may be disposed to favour him with a call after one o'clock. Our conversation was, as I have said, a long one,—naturally so, considering the highly interesting and important nature of the communication I was honoured by permission to make to him, and—and—and the numerous points which presented themselves for discussion. My friend the Marchese will naturally be interested in a detailed account of the manner in which—to the best of my poor ability—I discharged the commission, which my gracious—with which, I would say, my friend the Marchese Malatesta honoured me. And I shall have much pleasure in making such a detailed report at some future time of greater leisure. For the present, taking into consideration the anxiety which it is, perhaps, I may say natural,—though it is impossible to lose sight of the fact, that the social position of the Marchese Malatesta"—(with a bow and a smile that showed a whole *ratelier* of brilliant false teeth)—"ought to put all such anxiety out of the question; yet taking, I say, such a desire to hear the result of my conversation with the Signor Canonico into consideration, it may, perhaps, be more agreeable to my friend the Marchese that I should communicate to him in an epitomised, and, perhaps I may be allowed to say, condensed form, the substance of my—I may say—ambassorial negotiations."

And there the Marchese Florimond paused, looking from one to the other of the young men, with the pleased consciousness that he was making himself superlatively agreeable, and at the same time exhibiting his distinguished fitness for the highest and most delicate functions of diplomacy.

"That's it, uncle!" said Carlo, nodding encouragement. "Condense highly! and out with it!"

"I have the Marchese's permission to be abruptly brief?" said the little man, looking winningly into Malatesta's face.

"Certainly! By all means!" said Giulio, whose torture on the tenter-hooks of suspense had lasted almost to the limits of his endurance.

"It becomes my duty, then, to tell you, Signor

Marchese,—as I trust you will believe me when I say it is my pleasure,—that my friend—I may indeed without impropriety say, my *intimate* friend—the Canonico Adalberto, on hearing, not without considerable—yes! I do not feel myself at liberty to conceal from you, without *very considerable*—surprise, the circumstances which I was authorised to communicate to him; and on having satisfied himself by an amount of cross-questioning, which I *must* take the liberty of considering, and indeed of calling—at least among ourselves, if the Marchese will permit me to say so, and on the present occasion—singularly searching and severe, that there is—to put it bluntly and in vulgar language—no mistake about the matter;—the Canonico Adalberto, I say, then, and not before, declared, that it would be perfectly in accordance with his views and wishes to accord the hand of the Contessina Stella Altamari, his ward, to my valued friend the Marchese Giulio Malatesta."

"Pooh!" grunted Carlo, and "Ah!" sighed Giulio, with a sound like that of men drawing breath after having had their heads under water.

"I *think*," added the Marchese Florimond, looking inquiringly from one of the young men to the other, "that I am right in conceiving *that* to have been—putting aside for the present, in consideration of the press of circumstances, all those minor points, of which I reserve a detailed discussion for a more convenient opportunity,—the main scope, and, as I may say, aim of my mission."

"Hit it in the centre of the bull's eye! my dear uncle, as your matchless tact and skill always does! And now you had better take Giulio at once to the Canon!" said Carlo. "I told you it would be all plain sailing!" he added, turning to Giulio. But the injudicious observation was very near bringing down upon them another shower of the Marchese's choicest rhetoric.

"Not altogether, it is perhaps right, and I may say due to myself, to mention, such plain sailing, as you somewhat coarsely term it——" he began.

"Plain sailing, with such a pilot as you, uncle! Assuredly not otherwise, as I am sure Giulio is well aware. Off with you to the Canonico. I will wait for you here till you come back."

The Marchese felt himself rather unfairly curtailed in the enjoyment to which he considered himself honestly entitled in the matter; but being thus drummed out, went off with Giulio without further resistance, fully purposing to indemnify himself at the coming interview with the Canonico.

They found that distinguished churchman evidently waiting for them in his luxuriously furnished study.

"Signor Canonico," said the Marchese Florimond, as they entered, "I have the pleasure, and I request that you will believe that it is a very great pleasure——"

"Yes! I am sure of it! It is a pleasure also to me to make the acquaintance of the Marchese Giulio Malatesta," said the Canon, stepping forward gracefully, and offering his hand to Giulio, who took it, bowing rather stiffly.

"The extraordinary, and perhaps I may even say unparalleled——"

"Yes! indeed!" said the Canon, remorselessly, interrupting the tortured little Marchese, "the circumstances which the Marchese has related to me—and clearly substantiated—are indeed singular. We have but to shape the course of our duty to them."

"Such, I doubt not, will be the sentiments of my friend; and, if I may be permitted——"

But it was evident that the Canonico had no intention of permitting anything of the sort.

"Undoubtedly! we must all feel alike in this matter. You, Signor Marchese, are a soldier, and therefore know what *duty* is. We—soldiers under another banner—are equally its bounden lieges. I had, and have a duty to perform towards my niece, the Contessa Stella Altamari. I deemed it for her welfare to contract an alliance for her with the son and heir of the Marchese Cesare Malatesta. I still deem it so. My niece is reluctant, as young girls in their inexperience often are, to fall in with my views. She did not fancy the gentleman, who was supposed to hold the position which I considered a desirable one for her husband to occupy. And it became my duty to constrain her obedience. It was a very unpleasant duty. She *does* fancy"—(with a smile and bow such as only a polished and dignified churchman can execute)—"as I am given to understand, the gentleman who, most unexpectedly, is found to be the real holder of that position. And my duty becomes a pleasant one."

"I have the extreme happiness, then, Signor Canonico, of understanding that I may ask in marriage the hand of the Contessina Stella, with the approbation of her family?"

"Unquestionably so, my dear sir; with the full approbation of her family, and I trust I need not doubt with that of yours also."

"The very remarkable circumstances which I have had the good fortune, and I may, perhaps, say——" once again began the unhappy Marchese Florimond; but the Canonico Adalberto was too much for him.

"Exactly so! my dear Marchese!" he said; "I was on the point of asking the Marchese Malatesta whether any communication had taken place between him and his father since these circumstances were brought to light?"

"Not directly between me and my father," said Giulio; "but——"

"I trust, my dear sir," interrupted the Marchese Florimond, "that you will not think I acted injudiciously in so doing; but, as an old, and I may say, perhaps, valued friend of the family into which the Marchese Alfonso was about to marry, I thought it advisable to let the Marchese Cesare Malatesta know that some singular circumstances had arisen, which appeared to make his immediate presence in Florence desirable."

"It is probable, then, that we may shortly see him here," said the Canon.

"Besides," said Giulio, "the whole circumstances of the case will have been formally communicated to him before this by the legal gentleman I employed at Bologna."

"That is well!" said the Canonico; "you will probably," he added, "think it *proper* to communicate what you have now done me the honour of telling me, to the Contessa Zenobia;—and, you will, perhaps, think it *pleasant*," continued the Canon, smiling at his antithesis, "to make a similar communication to the younger lady."

Giulio bowed, but the Marchese gave him no chance of speaking.

"I purpose, with my friend the Marchese's good leave," he said, "presenting him to the Contessa Zenobia this evening. Signor Giulio is already a well known and valued acquaintance in Palazzo Altamari; but I shall have the pleasure of presenting him now for the first time in, as I may say, his proper person."

"Adieu, then, my dear sir, for the present!" said the Canon; "we shall meet again to talk our matters over more formally, when your excellent father shall have arrived here."

"*Addio*, Signor Canonico!"

"Well!" cried Carlo, meeting his uncle and Giulio at the door, as they returned from their important visit, "you found I was right in telling you there would be no difficulty, eh? All went well!"

"Humph!" grunted the Marchese Florimond, who was by no means in his usual good humour, "that *animalaccio* of a Canonico gets worse and worse! Positively there is no bearing him! A priest will be always a priest, polish him and varnish him as you will! No more breeding than a peasant! Thank Heaven, my dear Marchese, that when once you have married our Contessina, you need have nothing more to do with that intolerable old bore!"

"Priests will be priests! *Che volete!*" * said

* "What would you have?"

Carlo, winking at Malatesta; "but as to the business in hand, there was no difficulty, eh?"

"Difficulty! no, of course not! What difficulty should there be? And if the old fool" (he was not above twenty years younger than the Marchese Florimond) "would only have allowed me to state the case to him, it would all have been settled in half the time. But he took the words out of my mouth in the rudest manner! interrupted me again and again! and went on prosing and prosing, as if he were preaching a Lenten sermon, *per Bacco*, till his long-winded rigmarole made me positively sick! If it had not been for the sake of my friend the Marchese here, I should have turned my back on him, and walked out! There is nothing I abominate like a long-winded proser, who *will* speak, and then is so delighted with the sound of his own voice that he can't bring himself to stop!"

The little Marchese remained in happy unconsciousness of the whole salvo of winks with which his doleances were received by his undutiful nephew.

"This evening, then," said Carlo, "Giulio will make his proposals in due form to the Contessa Zenobia?"

"If the Signor Marchese is not too much disgusted with the annoyances my affairs have already caused him, and will kindly present me to La Signora Contessa."

"It will be a great pleasure to me to do so, my dear sir! And I flatter myself—yes, I really *may* be allowed to say I *do* flatter myself—that our interview with the Contessa Zenobia will be of a more agreeable, and perhaps it would hardly be going too far to say a more *convenable*, kind than that which has just passed with that ill-bred priest."

"Hang him! We'll think no more about him!" said Carlo. "At what o'clock shall we be here to accompany you to the Palazzo Altamari, uncle?"

"Say at nine! I have an engagement after dinner that I cannot excuse myself from."

"At nine we will be here! Come along, Giulio!"

At the hour named the three gentlemen proceeded to the Palazzo Altamari, and by a little management on the part of the Marchese were received by the Contessa Zenobia alone in her *boudoir*.

"Signora Contessa!" said the Marchese, with an air that might have formed a study for the "introducer of ambassadors" to Louis the Fourteenth, "I have the honour, and am sure you will attach to my words all their full significance when I add the great pleasure, of presenting to you the

Marchese Giulio Malatesta, dei Marchesi Malatesta di Fermo."

Giulio bowed very gracefully, and looked very handsome as he did so, which the Marchese Florimond felt was very creditable to him, the Marchese Florimond.

"*Dieu de ma vie! Marquis!*" screamed the brisk little lady; "*qu'est ce que vous me chantez là!* I have had the pleasure of knowing this gentleman before; and, *foi de Biron!* it would have been a pleasure if he had not given us all such a deal of botheration about Stella! You are a dangerous man, Monsieur Mauvaisetête! He! he! he! positively a member of the *classes dangereuses, parbleu!* You go about stealing ladies' hearts! *Passe pour cela!* But you want to steal their hands too, which, *la Sainte Vierge me garde!* is quite another matter. I do not know what the Canonico will say if he catches you here!"

"I am here, *Gentilissima Signora Contessa*," said Giulio, smiling, "with the permission of the Signor Canonico, for the purpose of asking you to give me that, which you accuse me of wishing to steal!"

"With the permission of the Canonico! *Diable!* And *pardon! Monsieur Mauvaisetête;* but what is this that our friend here the Marchese is saying? I thought that you were—you know!—*Je suis sans préjugés moi! Ma foi!*—I thought you were *Monsieur Mauvaisetête, des Mauvaisetêtes*, as one may say, after a fashion; but he calls you the Marquis Mauvaisetête!"

"Permit me, *Ornatissima Signora Contessa*," said the Marchese Florimond, with a flourish of his white hand, "to explain the circumstances, which seem to your singularly lucid intelligence and unerring discernment to involve a certain degree of difficulty, which, I may perhaps be allowed to say, without unduly exaggerating my meaning, almost—*almost* I say—reach the limits of inexplicability."

The Marchese drew breath, changed his attitude, and prepared for a new exordium.

"Cut along! Marquis!" said the Contessa Zenobia.

"My uncle hates long-winded prosing in others too much to be ever long himself!" said Carlo, with a look at Giulio.

"The Marchese Malatesta, *Gentilissima Signora Contessa*, whose name you so felicitously translate into the favoured language of which you are so perfect and so graceful a mistress, is, as I have had the honour of telling you, and as I am about to have, if you will kindly permit me, that of satisfactorily—yes! I *may* say—I *think* I may say;—nay, assuredly I MAY say, satisfactorily convincing you—ay, CONVINCING you, no other than the Marchese Giulio Malatesta, dei Malatesta, the heir to the present Marchese Cesare, and the representative of that ancient and very illustrious family."

And then the Marchese Florimond, with an intense enjoyment, which really he deserved after the snubbing of the Canonico, proceeded to tell the story he had to tell, with an amplitude of that special rhetorical adornment of which he was so great a master, but which may be more advantageously perhaps,—nay, I may surely be allowed to say certainly,—more advantageously left to the imagination of the reader. He asked special permission for the use of each epithet, doubted, weighed the question, and finally decided in his own favour, respecting the exact force of every adverb, and availed himself to the utmost of every periphrasis provided by the wordy forms of Italian courtesy. Giulio devoutly wished that the Canonico Adalberto had been there to dam the torrent, as he had so ably done that morning. At last, however, the Marchese brought his story reluctantly to an end; and the Contessa Zenobia, who had listened to it with unexampled patience for her, cried:

"*Che Kyrie-eleeson!* * What a story! *Par tous*

* The Greek words, "*κυριε ελεησον*," recurring again and again with wearisome repetition in the litanies and other services of the Roman Catholic Church, are often irreverently used by Italians to signify any tedious long rigmarole.

les saints et tous les diables, there has been nothing like it since the *Conspiration des Fous contre les Médecins,* that Stella was reading about in her history of Florence this morning!"

"Excuse me, Signora Contessa, if I confess that I see neither madmen nor physicians in this matter," said the Marchese Florimond in considerable perplexity.

"What on earth has she got into that high-dried old brain of hers now!" muttered Carlo aside to Giulio; "*Conspiration des Fous contre les Médecins!* What can she mean?"

"Ah! I have it!" said Giulio in the same tone. "The Signora Contessa," he went on aloud, "is alluding to the Conspiracy of the *Pazzi* against the *Medici!*"

"*Parbleu!* It's clear, I think! You and I, Monsieur le Marquis Mauvaisetête, understand each other, *n'est ce pas!*"

"There must have been a conspiracy of the kind she spoke of, I think, when she was allowed to go at large!" said Carlo aside to his friend.

"I hope sincerely that we may always do so!" said Giulio, bowing low to the Contessa.

"I am sure we shall! *Pardi!* It's a mercy that dear Stella will escape that poor little apology for a man, the Marquis Alphonse! I must own that the little puss knew how to choose for herself!

He! He! He! But you've given us a terrible time of it; you and she between you! He!

C'est l'amour, l'amour, l'amour,
Que fait le monde à la ronde!

N'est ce pas, Monsieur de Mauvaisetête. And now I suppose you would like to see La Stellina, and tell her all about it."

And so Stella, greatly wondering, was summoned from her up-stairs exile, and the *boudoir* was, contrary to all Italian precedent, left to her and Giulio, while La Contessa went to receive her evening *habitués.*

Infinitely greater still was Stella's surprise, when she found that the object for which she had been sent for on this last evening before her departure for the new convent, was to have a *tête-à-tête* with Giulio in her aunt's boudoir.

"You have not made any promises, my Giulio?" said she, turning pale after their first passionate greeting; "you have not bought this interview at the price of any concessions!"

"I've made no promises, darling, save those which I am ready to renew to you; and I am here to ask and not to make concessions!"

And then he told her all the strange story, which accounted for his presence there, and for the change in their prospects.

"I hope it won't make you grow like any of the

other Marcheses I know," said Stella, playfully pouting and looking fondly into his face the while, after the first wonder of the extraordinary tidings had been discussed, a happy tear or two been shed, and the new position in which Giulio stood towards his love had been recognised, and the rights pertaining thereto claimed and duly admitted.

"What! not like the Marchese Florimond, for example, or the Marchese Alfonso!" said Giulio, with mock astonishment.

"*I* won't call you Marchese!" said Stella, "that I promise you! But tell me, my Giulio, all about your mother, your dear mother, who was dear to me before she was dear to you!"

"Yes! my Stella! I know all about it! It is written in my destiny that no good thing shall come to me save through and by you! I heard of your generous, dear insistance that my mother should make herself known to me! My poor, dear mother! She was so sensitively fearful! The dread lest, what she then thought her equivocal position, should be a disadvantage to me—to us, was so paramount! 'Stella insisted on it!' she said. 'She knew all my unhappy story, and yet she insisted on it!' Ah! what a pleasure it was to put all such timid misgivings to flight for ever!"

"It must, indeed, have been a meeting to remember for ever, my Giulio! Were you able to see her alone?"

"No! there was an old nun in the room all the time! She went fast asleep, though. But, oh! Stella, there happened the most absurd scene! You would have laughed to such a degree——!"

"Laughed! I should not have guessed that there had been anything to laugh at!" said Stella, opening wide her beautiful eyes.

"You shall judge! But it is impossible to make you understand the scene without acting it! There is nothing like a diagram for rightly explaining positions!"

"A diagram, Giulio, what is that?" inquired Stella, innocently.

"You shall see! We had come to the end of our mutual explanations, and it was time to separate, for Carlo was waiting outside the convent to take me to my interview with your uncle. There sat, or knelt rather, the old nun fast asleep over her beads—there, we will suppose, close to that door. It is a pity we have nobody to represent her part! You must fancy her there;—quite fast asleep, you know! My mother, who was sitting, as it might be, just where you are sitting, got up. (You must stand up.) I got up, too—thus! My mother put her arms up—so! (You must do it for the right understanding of what followed.)

I, of course, caught her to my breast—like this. She locked me tight in her arms! (You won't catch the joke if the diagram is not complete!) —That is correct! We were just——"

"No! sir! be quiet, Giulio! One diagram is quite enough!"

"—just so, when looking up, we saw——By Jove, the diagram *is* complete!" cried Giulio, bursting into a loud laugh. For, at that moment, as they both looked up, there was standing, just where the nun should have stood, Mademoiselle Zélie, who, not having heard anything of the sudden change in the Altamari politics, exhibited all the horror requisite to the due presentment of her part in Giulio's little drama. Unlike the original performer, however, she did not stand her ground, but rushed screaming, as if the house had been in flames, into the adjoining room, where, fortunately, no strangers had yet arrived to join the Contessa Zenobia and the Marchese and Carlo.

"Gracious Heavens! What has happened? What is the matter?" cried the Contessa.

"*C'est trop fort! c'est une infamie!* I saw it with my eyes!" screamed Mademoiselle Zélie!

"Mademoiselle, I beg, and if I may be permitted the use of such an expression, I *adjure* you, to tell us *what* you have seen?" said the Marchese Florimond.

"Will *you* tell us, Monsieur de Mauvaisetête, what on earth is the matter?" said the Contessa, turning to Giulio, as he and Stella followed the outraged duenna into the room.

"Evidently something which Mademoiselle Zélie has never seen before!" said Giulio, looking at Carlo with a laugh in his eye.

"He was only showing me a diagram, aunt!" said Stella, very demurely.

"A what! child?" asked the Contessa.

"I *saw* him KISS Mademoiselle!" exclaimed the exasperated Zélie, savagely.

"And they call that a diagram, now-a-days, do they?" said the Contessa Zenobia. "*Que de nouvelles modes! Mais—pourvu que la chose reste toujours la même! n'est ce pas, Monsieur de Mauvaisetête!*"

CHAPTER VII.

CONCLUSION.

HAVING followed the fortunes of Giulio Malatesta to the culminating point attained in the last chapter, it will scarcely be deemed necessary by the lads and lasses—the "*virgines puerique,*" for whose benefit we nineteenth-century *trouvères* mainly indite our romaunts—that the sequel of them should be traced in detail:

Ich habe genossen das irdische Glück
Ich habe gelebt und geliebet.

'Tis the consummation! the Pisgah-top, from which a long-stretching vista of tranquil happiness, a whole promised land of peaceful fruition may be seen, but which shall be equalled in its glory by no one spot of the smiling country to be traversed.

Not that the after-stretches of the road are not

often exceedingly pleasant travelling. But we don't gallop, and bound, and shy, and bolt over them in a manner so interesting to others travelling the road. Our pleasant progress is more after the fashion somewhat disdainfully termed by ardent youth, jog-trot; the history of which may with advantage be very compendiously told.

The Marchese and Marchesa Malatesta-Altamari—(for the Canonico Adalberto succeeded in causing that collocation of the names to be adopted)—would be admitted by the most exclusive admirers of domestic felicity after our own dear island pattern, to be as happy a couple as the sun shines on. They have two children, a boy and a girl. And the boy is named, strangely enough, as many people have thought, not Giulio, nor Cesare, nor Adalberto, but Pietro; as if he were called, not after his relatives, but after his tutor, the Professor Pietro Varani, sometime of the University of Pisa. The little girl, a lovely child, is called Maddalena.

There remains one fact of a tragic nature to be told in connexion with the events that have been narrated; a circumstance which was surrounded with so much of mystery and strangeness, that it might of itself furnish forth the materials for a story of Italian life that would not be without interest, but which may here be told with the utmost possible brevity, as a notable instance of that retribution of circumstances which events work out more frequently, perhaps, in countries less liegely subject to law than our own.

The Marchese Cesare Malatesta never arrived in Florence. It was very soon proved, however, that he started from Fermo for the former city on the receipt of the letter from the Marchese Florimond, which the reader has seen. It appeared, also, that the news of the declared validity of the Bologna marriage had reached Fermo from Bologna, and had become known in the former city some days previously to the departure of the Marchese from Fermo. That time of the re-establishment of all the old Papal despotism, after the brief gleam of a better state of things, was a period of much lawlessness and violence. The ecclesiastical states, especially the more southern portions of them, were infested by numerous bands of desperate men, who, feeling that the world and the world's law was not their friend, recurred readily to the old Italian remedy of brigandage. Such a band was known to be at that time in the mountains in the neighbourhood of Fermo. And when the two servants who were travelling with the Marchese Cesare, came back declaring that the carriage had been stopped, and their master shot dead, after being robbed, by a number of men with crape over their faces, it was accepted as a self-evident fact that he

www.ingramcontent.com/pod-product-compliance
Lightning Source LLC
Chambersburg PA
CBHW021217270326
41929CB00010B/1165
* 9 7 8 3 3 3 7 0 2 7 8 0 3 *